Office for National Statistics
Social Survey Division

Smoking among secondary school children in 1996: England

An enquiry carried out by Social Survey Division of ONS

on behalf of the Department of Health

Lindsey Jarvis

London: The Stationery Office

Contents

Acknowledgements

Social surveys are always the work of a team. The author takes full responsibility for the content of this report, but gratefully acknowledges the contribution of specialist colleagues who carried out the fieldwork and editing stages of the survey.

The author would like to thank the education authorities and the schools for their co-operation and, perhaps most important of all, the pupils who took part in the survey.

Definitions and notes to tables

Classification of smoking behaviour

The fivefold classification used in this series of surveys is based on a combination of information from the self-completion questionnaire and the smoking diary. Saliva cotinine concentrations have not been used to modify the classification since these data are available for only a quarter of the sample in England.

Pupils who indicated on the questionnaire that they smoked at least one cigarette a week were classified as regular smokers, irrespective of the numbers of cigarettes recorded on the diary or whether, indeed, they had recorded any cigarettes at all.

Similarly, pupils who were current smokers but said that they usually smoked less than one cigarette a week were classified as occasional smokers, irrespective of the number of cigarettes on the diary, or whether they had recorded any cigarettes at all. In addition, those who had indicated on the questionnaire that they were not current smokers but who had recorded cigarettes on the diary were also classified as occasional smokers, irrespective of the number of cigarettes recorded.

Those who were not current smokers and who had not recorded any cigarettes on the diary were classified according to their responses on the questionnaire as used to smoke, tried smoking once, or never smoked.

Further information about the derivation of the classification can be found in Appendix B.

Age

In tables where age is a variable, those aged 16 have been included with the 15 year olds. This is because the survey did not include pupils in year 12, and the small number of 16 year olds sampled from year 11 are not representative of all schoolchildren aged 16.

School Year

The classification is based on the years or forms of maintained secondary schools. The school years of pupils attending middle and upper schools and some non-maintained schools have been adjusted accordingly.

Since the introduction of the National Curriculum in England and Wales, education authorities have been advised to number school years consecutively through from the first year at primary school to the last year at secondary school. This means that what used to be the first form in a secondary school is now year 7, the second form is now year 8, and so on. Since 1993 the survey uses the new system of year numbering and, accordingly, refers to years 7 through 11 (equivalent of the old first to fifth form).

Region

Four broad regional groupings are shown, as follows :

North	North, Yorkshire & Humberside, North West
Midlands	East Midlands, West Midlands, East Anglia
	(and Wales in 1982, 1984, and 1986)
South	South East, South West,
Greater London	

Notes to tables

1. A few children failed to answer each question. These 'no answers' have been excluded from the analysis, and so tables that describe the same population may have slightly varying bases.

2. Percentages based on fewer than 50 cases are shown in brackets because of the relatively large sampling errors attached to small numbers.

3. The following convention has been used

0 = nil or less than 0.5%
- = not applicable

Summary of main findings

The main purpose of this survey was to continue to monitor trends in prevalence of regular cigarette smoking (defined as usually smoking at least one cigarette a week) among secondary school children aged 11-15 in England.

Prevalence of cigarette smoking (Chapter 2)
In 1996, 13% of those aged 11-15 in England were regular smokers (defined as usually smoking at least one cigarette a week). Although the increase in prevalence between 1994 and 1996 from 12% to 13% was not statistically significant, it continues the recent upward trend.

Throughout the 1990s, girls have been more likely to smoke than boys - 15% of girls and 11% of boys were regular smokers in 1996.

The proportion of pupils smoking rises with age and progress through the school. Very few children are smokers when they start secondary school, but, by the time they are 15 years old, three in ten pupils are regular smokers.

Amount smoked (Chapter 2)
In 1996, the mean number of cigarettes recorded in the diary week by regular smokers was 56 for boys and 47 for girls. Although this difference was not statistically significant, it replicates previous findings that boys are heavier smokers than girls.

The majority of regular smokers, 70%, had smoked more than 20 cigarettes in the previous week: indeed a quarter smoked, on average, at least ten cigarettes a day.

The mean number of cigarettes smoked per pupil in the previous week has remained broadly similar over the last few surveys and, in 1996, the mean per pupil was 7.

Dependence on smoking (Chapter 2)
About two-thirds, 65%, of regular smokers said that it would be difficult to go without smoking for a week and three-quarters reported that they would find it difficult to give up altogether.

Although girls were more likely than boys to have tried to give up, they were no more likely to want to give up than boys.

Those who had been smoking regularly for longer than a year were more likely to feel dependent than those who had not been smoking that long.

Purchase of cigarettes (Chapter 3)
A quarter (25%) of all pupils tried to purchase cigarettes from a shop in the last year. Of these pupils, 38% had been refused at least once in the last year.

As in previous years the majority of pupils, 89%, bought cigarettes from a shop rather than buying them from a machine or being given them by friends.

Smoking and the family (Chapter 4)
Children were much more likely to be smokers if other people at home smoked. Brothers and sisters appeared to have more influence in this respect than did parents - pupils with brothers or sisters who smoked were much more likely than other pupils to be smokers, irrespective of the smoking behaviour of their parents.

Overall those who had at least one brother or sister who smoked were over four times as likely to be smokers themselves as were those who said none of their brothers or sisters smoked.

Most pupils said that their families disapproved (or would disapprove) of their smoking. Nearly half of all current smokers said that their families did not know they smoked.

Children's attitudes to smoking (Chapter 5)
An overwhelming majority of pupils agreed with the attitude statements about the adverse consequences of smoking, especially those concerning health risks. Thus, 98% of pupils agreed with the statement 'Smoking can cause lung cancer'. As in 1994, pupils were much less likely to agree with statements about the possible positive benefits of smoking. Indeed, there was a shift towards less agreement with these 'positive' statements between 1994 and 1996. For example, the proportion who agreed that smokers stayed slimmer than non-smokers fell from 24% to 21%.

Pupils' attitudes to the negative statements did not vary according to their smoking behaviour. However, smokers were more likely to think that statements about the perceived positive effects of smoking were true.

Health education (Chapter 6)
Children receive information about the health risks of smoking from a variety of sources. In the past year over half of all children had discussed the health risks of smoking with someone in their family. Over two thirds of pupils remembered receiving a lesson about smoking at school.

1 Introduction

1.1 Background to the survey

This was the ninth national survey of smoking among secondary schoolchildren and was carried out in England and Scotland at the request of the Department of Health and the Scottish Office Department of Health. The results of the survey in Scotland are discussed in a separate report.[1]

The first of this series of surveys was carried out in 1982, to provide estimates of the proportion of pupils who smoked, and to describe the smoking behaviour of those who did smoke. Similar surveys have been carried out every two years since then to provide further estimates from which trends in the prevalence of cigarette smoking among secondary schoolchildren can be monitored.

Recent surveys, including an additional survey conducted only in England in 1993, have also been used to measure progress towards the 1994 *Health of the Nation*[2] target for children's smoking in England. The target set out in the White Paper published in 1992 was to reduce smoking prevalence among 11-15 year olds by at least 33% by 1994 from a 1988 baseline figure of 8%. The 1994 survey in this series found that the target had not been reached and that the prevalence of smoking in this age group had risen to 12%.

The aim of the 1996 survey, based on independent samples for England and Scotland was to continue the series of estimates of prevalence of cigarette smoking among secondary schoolchildren and to draw attention to any changes in behaviour.

The content of the 1996 survey was similar to that of previous years with the addition of some questions asking pupils about consumer durables in their home, the number of cars their family had and whether their home was owned or rented, to be used as indicators of their family's socio-economic position. Questions about educational expectations were also asked for the first time. As in previous surveys, saliva specimens were collected from half the sample. These were analysed for the presence of cotinine, a metabolite of nicotine, which is a measure of exposure to tobacco smoke. The main purpose of this was to enable some validation to be made of the self-reported smoking data. As in 1994 the survey included some questions about children's drinking behaviour. The results from this part of the survey will be published separately.[3, 4]

1.2 Sample coverage

Estimates of smoking prevalence were required for the population of secondary school pupils in England.

The population covered by the survey in England was pupils in years 7 to 11 (previously called first to fifth formers); that is, mainly pupils who were aged 11 to 15 at the start of the school year in September 1996.

The survey covered pupils attending all types of maintained secondary schools, including middle schools with pupils aged 11 or over, and non-maintained secondary schools, except special schools.

1.3 Design of the survey

A two-stage sample design was used. At the first stage a sample of schools was drawn, and at the second stage a sample of pupils was selected within each school. A list of secondary schools was extracted from the 1996 school database supplied by the School's Register for the Department for Education and Employment. The list of schools was stratified by type of school, whether single sex or mixed, and region.

A sample of 128 schools was selected with probability proportional to the number of pupils aged 11-15. This type of sample design enabled equal numbers of pupils to be selected for interview from each school. Further details of the sample are given in Appendix A.

Saliva specimens were collected from all pupils in half the sample of schools. Although it is not ideal to have all the pupils in one school allocated to either the saliva or non-saliva sample, because of the effect of clustering in the sample design, this is more practicable than collecting specimens from half the selected pupils in each school.

All the schools selected were approached (with the permission of their education authorities in the case of LEA maintained schools) and asked if they would be willing to take part in the survey. Each of the co-operating schools was then visited by an ONS interviewer who selected a systematic sample of pupils taken from all the school registers for years 7 to 11 inclusive.

Each school was given copies of a letter from ONS to be sent to parents of the selected children, telling them about the survey, and asking them to reply only if they wished their child not to take part.

The sampled pupils were brought together in a classroom under the supervision of an interviewer but with no teacher present. They were each asked to complete two documents :

1 a questionnaire about current smoking behaviour and other topics.

2 a diary in which they were asked to record all cigarettes smoked during the previous seven days.

In those schools where saliva specimens were to be obtained, pupils were asked to put a small dental roll in their mouth, between the cheek and the lower gum, and keep it there for about twenty minutes while they completed the questionnaire. Pupils were fully aware of the purpose of the procedure and were told that both smokers and non-smokers would have nicotine in their saliva.

Care was taken to protect the confidentiality of pupils' answers and to make them aware that their answers would not be identified with them personally, nor with the school. Questionnaires, diaries, and saliva specimens were linked by means of a serial number only; names were not used on any of the documents.

If four or more pupils were absent at the main visit, the interviewer made a follow-up visit to the school several days later, if possible checking beforehand that pupils who were absent at the main visit were back in school.

1.4 Response

Information was obtained from 2854 pupils in the 111 co-operating schools, 87% of those selected for interview. Taking into account non-response among eligible schools as well as among pupils in co-operating schools, the overall response rate was 78%.

The saliva test did not appear to have an effect on school response; equal numbers of saliva and non-saliva schools refused to take part in the

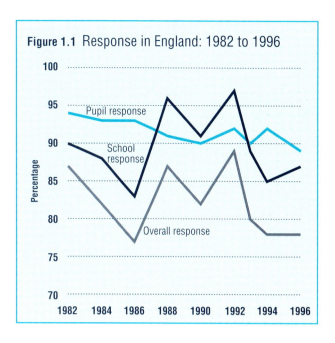

Figure 1.1 Response in England: 1982 to 1996

survey. The most common reasons given by head teachers for not taking part in the survey were that they had recently participated in other surveys, or that their school was going to be inspected.

Table 1.1

The response rate for schools was slightly higher than in 1994 but the pupil response rate was at its lowest level in this series of surveys.

Figure 1.1

References

1. Barton J and Jarvis L. *Smoking among secondary school children in 1996: Scotland* , 1997 (London: The Stationery Office)

2. *The Health of the Nation*, 1992 (London: HMSO)

3. Goddard E. *Young teenagers and alcohol in 1996 Volume 1: England* (in press)

4. Goddard E. *Young teenagers and alcohol in 1996 Volume 2: Scotland* (in press)

Table 1.1 Summary of response rates

England 1996

	Saliva		Non saliva		Total	
	No.	%	No.	%	No.	%
Schools sampled	64		64		128	
Ineligible schools*			1		1	
Eligible schools	64		63		127	
Co-operating schools	56	88	55	87	111	87
Number of pupils selected	1620	100	1578	100	3198	100
Pupils interviewed	1434	89	1420	90	2854	89
Total non-response	186	11	158	10	344	11
absent, sick	48		45		93	
absent, truant	13		11		24	
absent, unknown	40		45		85	
refusal by pupil	33		16		49	
refusal by parent	14		6		20	
other	38		35		73	
Overall response rate (allowing for non-response of schools and pupils)		77%		79%		78%

* One school had closed

2 Smoking prevalence and consumption

2.1 Health of the Nation Target

The Health of the Nation[1] target for children's smoking set for 1994 was to reduce the prevalence of regular cigarette smoking (defined as usually smoking one or more cigarettes a week) among 11-15 year olds by at least 33% from the 1988 baseline figure of 8%.

The 1994 survey in this series found that the target had not been reached and that the prevalence of smoking in this age group had risen to 12%. In 1996, prevalence rose again to 13% but this increase on the 1994 figure was not statistically significant.

As discussed in the 1994 report, it would appear that the 1988 results used as the baseline for the *Health of the Nation* targets were exceptionally low and gave a false expectation of likely future trends. The period in the early nineties, 1990 to 1993, during which prevalence remained stable at 10% has been followed by two increases in prevalence suggesting that the trend in children's smoking prevalence may now be upwards. This is despite the anti-smoking initiatives aimed at children such as the 1996 'Respect' campaign, commissioned by the Health Education Authority.

The increase in prevalence of children's smoking appears to be inconsistent with the trend in adult smoking, monitored by the General Household Survey which showed a decrease in the proportion aged 16 and over who smoked cigarettes from 30% to 27% between 1990 and 1994 (1996 figures are not yet available). This same decrease to 27% was found in the youngest age group monitored on the GHS although the difference was not statistically significant among those aged 16-19. However, the most recently published figures for smoking in the 1995 Health Survey for England suggest an upward trend among those aged 16-24. In 1993, 32% of men in this age group were smokers compared with 36% in 1995, and for women the proportion of smokers aged 16-24 increased from 32% to 37% in the same time period.

The increases for boys and girls separately between 1994 and 1996 were not statistically significant. However, the overall trend since 1993 has shown an increase in the proportion of

regular smokers for both sexes: from 8% in 1993 to 11% in 1996 for boys and from 11% to 15% for girls.

Girls continue to be more likely than boys to be regular smokers and the proportion of girls who smoke regularly is now the highest since the survey began in 1982. The increase between 1994 and 1996 in the proportion of girls who regularly smoke was accompanied by a decrease in the proportion of girls who had never smoked from 52% in 1994 to 48% in 1996.

Figure 2.1, Table 2.1

2.2 Prevalence of smoking behaviour in relation to age and school year

Earlier reports in this series have shown that the likelihood of a boy or girl smoking grows with age and progress through the school (these two factors being, of course, closely linked), and that of the two, age is the more important factor. Very few pupils are smokers when they start secondary school, but by 13 years old, one in ten pupils smokes regularly and by 15 years old, three in ten pupils smoke regularly.

Figure 2.2, Table 2.2

In 1996, among 14 year-olds, girls were almost twice as likely to be regular smokers as boys of the same age (24% of girls compared with 13% of boys). There were no statistically significant changes in prevalence rates for each age between 1994 and 1996 for either sex.

Table 2.3

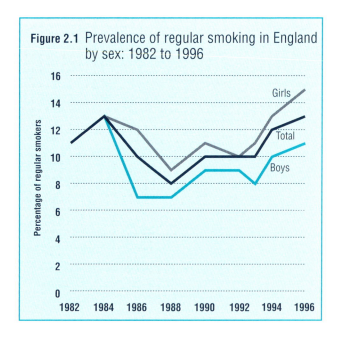

Figure 2.1 Prevalence of regular smoking in England by sex: 1982 to 1996

2.3 Regional variation in smoking behaviour

Regional variations in smoking behaviour are difficult to interpret because the small sample size in each region, and the clustering of the sample in schools, lead to high sampling errors. The problem is partially overcome by grouping the regions into larger areas.

Although there was a higher level of smoking prevalence in the North compared with the South in 1996 (15% compared with 10%), the surveys have shown no consistent pattern of regional variation in smoking behaviour during the 14 year period in which they have been carried out. The only statistically significant change in smoking prevalence in the four regions was an increase in the North from 10% of pupils in 1994 to 15% in 1996.

Table 2.4

2.4 Cigarette consumption according to the diary

Cigarette consumption was measured by summing the number of cigarettes recorded on the diary as being smoked on each day of the previous week.

The majority of regular smokers, 70%, had recorded more than 20 cigarettes in the diary: indeed a quarter had recorded more than seventy a week, averaging at least ten cigarettes smoked a day. Only three per cent of regular smokers had not smoked in the previous week compared with 20% of occasional smokers. More

than half, 53%, of occasional smokers had smoked between one and five cigarettes during the diary week. Two per cent of those who said they were occasional smokers had recorded smoking on average at least ten cigarettes a day.

Among regular smokers, there was no significant difference between boys and girls in the proportions who smoked at least ten cigarettes a day (25% of boys and 23% of girls).

Table 2.5 also shows the mean and median numbers of cigarettes recorded by regular and occasional smokers. These averages are based on all regular and occasional smokers, including those who recorded no cigarettes on the diary. The median number of cigarettes is also presented, since a few pupils record a large number of cigarettes on the diary, and this has a disproportionate influence on the mean value.

Table 2.5

2.5 Trends in cigarette consumption

The pattern of cigarette consumption has remained broadly the same since the survey began, despite changes in prevalence levels. In 1996, the mean number of cigarettes smoked by regular smokers was very similar to that of the previous year: 56 for boys and 47 for girls. Although this difference between boys and girls was not statistically significant, boys have smoked a greater number of cigarettes, on average, than girls in every survey except 1984, and so the difference is unlikely to be due to fluctuations in the sample. The mean

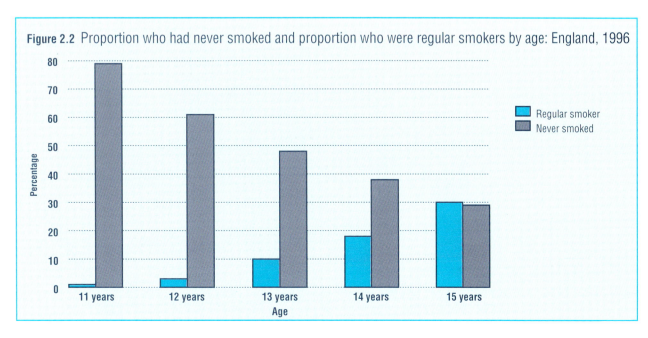

Figure 2.2 Proportion who had never smoked and proportion who were regular smokers by age: England, 1996

number of cigarettes smoked per pupil has continued to remain fairly constant: in 1996, the mean per pupil was 7, compared with 6 in 1994 (this increase was not statistically significant).

Table 2.6

2.6 Length of time as a smoker

Regular smokers were asked how long it was since they started smoking at least one cigarette a week. In 1996, over two-thirds, 67%, said that they had been doing so for more than one year compared with 57% of regular smokers in 1994. There was an increase among girls in those who had been smoking this long from 54% in 1994 to 65% in 1996, but the increase among boys, from 61% in 1994 to 69% in 1996, was not statistically significant.

Table 2.7

2.7 Dependence on smoking

Regular smokers were asked a series of questions designed to give some indication of whether or not they were dependent on smoking. About two-thirds, 65%, felt that it would be difficult to go without smoking for a week, and about a third, 32%, reported they would find it very difficult. Three-quarters of regular smokers, 75%, said that they would find giving up difficult. There were very similar proportions of boys and girls in each category.

Girls were more likely than boys to have tried to give up smoking in the past (80% compared with 67%) but there was no significant difference in the proportions of boys and girls wanting to give up smoking.

Overall in 1996, 45% of regular smokers said they would like to give up smoking compared with 34% in 1994. There was also an increase in the proportion who had tried giving up smoking from 62% in 1994 to 75% in 1996.

Tables 2.8 - 2.9

Over half, 53%, of those who had tried to give up smoking in the past would still like to give up but almost one in ten were definite that they would not like to try again - perhaps because of their lack of success in the past. However, those who had tried to give up were still almost three times more likely to want to give up than those who had not tried (53% compared with 19%).

Table 2.10

As in 1994, the likelihood of feeling dependent was much greater among those who had been smoking regularly for more than a year than among those who had started smoking more recently, but was quite high even among the latter group. For example, 84% of those who had been regular smokers for more than a year would find it difficult to give up altogether, compared with 58% of those who had been smokers for a shorter time.

Part of the reason for the difference could be that the longer pupils have smoked, the more realistic is their assessment of the difficulty of giving up and the more likely they are to have tried to give up and failed (81% of longer term smokers had tried to give up compared with 60% of those smoking for one year or less).

However, there was no difference among those who had been smoking regularly for more than a year and those who had smoked for a shorter time in their wish to give up smoking (45% compared with 43%).

Figure 2.3, Table 2.11

As discussed in the 1994 report, the results of this survey suggested that girls may be dependent on smoking (or may think they are) at lower levels of nicotine intake. For example, girls who reported they would find it difficult not to smoke for a week smoked on average 60 cigarettes a week compared with an average of 72 cigarettes smoked by boys giving the same answer. These differences were not statistically significant, possibly because of the sample sizes, but as they replicated earlier findings they are unlikely to be due to fluctuations in the sample.

This apparent dependency in girls at lower levels of smoking may be due to physical and/or psychological dependence at a lower level of nicotine intake. There are, however, other possible explanations - for example, girls may be more prepared than boys to admit to concern about withdrawal symptoms, or they may be more likely than boys to think that admitting to being dependent makes them feel more grown up.

Tables 2.12-2.13

Reference

1. *The Health of the Nation.* HMSO (1992).

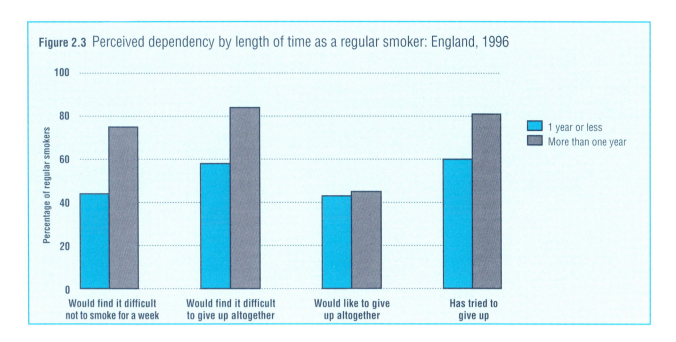

Figure 2.3 Perceived dependency by length of time as a regular smoker: England, 1996

Table 2.1   Smoking behaviour by sex: 1982 to 1996
All pupils   *England*

Smoking behaviour	1982	1984	1986	1988	1990	1992	1993	1994	1996
	%	%	%	%	%	%	%	%	%
Boys									
Regular smoker	11	13	7	7	9	9	8	10	11
Occasional smoker	7	9	5	5	6	6	7	9	8
Used to smoke	11	11	10	8	7	6	6	7	7
Tried smoking	26	24	23	23	22	22	22	21	22
Never smoked	45	44	55	58	56	57	57	53	53
Base(=100%)	*1460*	*1928*	*1676*	*1489*	*1643*	*1662*	*1613*	*1522*	*1445*
Girls									
Regular smoker	11	13	12	9	11	10	11	13	15
Occasional smoker	9	9	5	5	6	7	9	10	10
Used to smoke	10	10	10	9	7	7	10	8	9
Tried smoking	22	22	19	19	18	19	18	17	18
Never smoked	49	46	53	59	58	57	53	52	48
Base(=100%)	*1514*	*1689*	*1508*	*1529*	*1478*	*1626*	*1527*	*1523*	*1409*
Total									
Regular smoker	11	13	10	8	10	10	10	12	13
Occasional smoker	8	9	5	5	6	7	8	9	9
Used to smoke	10	10	10	8	7	7	8	8	8
Tried smoking	24	23	21	21	20	20	20	19	20
Never smoked	47	45	54	58	57	57	55	53	51
Base(=100%)	*2979*	*3658*	*3189*	*3018*	*3121*	*3295*	*3140*	*3045*	*2854*

Table 2.2   Smoking behaviour by age
All pupils   *England 1996*

Smoking behaviour	11 years	12 years	13 years	14 years	15 years	Total
Regular smoker	1	3	10	18	30	13
Occasional smoker	4	5	10	11	13	9
Used to smoke	2	7	11	14	7	8
Tried smoking	14	24	22	18	21	20
Never smoked	79	61	48	38	29	51
Base(=100%)	*546*	*575*	*560*	*586*	*587*	*2854*

Table 2.3 Proportion of pupils who were regular smokers by sex and age; by sex and school year: 1982 to 1996

All pupils   *England*

	1982	1984	1986	1988	1990	1992	1993	1994	1996	*1996 base (=100%)*
	Percentage who were regular smokers									
Boys										
Age										
aged 11	1	0	0	0	0	0	0	1	1	*272*
aged 12	2	2	2	2	2	2	3	2	2	*297*
aged 13	8	10	5	5	6	6	3	4	8	*282*
aged 14	18	16	6	8	10	14	14	14	13	*298*
aged 15	24	28	18	17	25	21	19	26	28	*296*
School year										
year 7	3	0	0	1	1	1	1	2	1	*324*
year 8	2	3	2	2	3	3	3	2	4	*281*
year 9	9	12	5	5	7	7	4	5	8	*280*
year 10	19	17	8	9	12	16	13	15	13	*289*
year 11	26	31	19	18	26	20	22	28	28	*271*
Girls										
Age										
aged 11	0	1	0	1	1	0	0	0	0	*274*
aged 12	1	2	2	0	2	2	3	3	4	*278*
aged 13	6	9	5	4	9	9	5	8	11	*278*
aged 14	14	19	16	12	16	15	18	20	24	*288*
aged 15	25	28	27	22	25	25	26	30	33	*291*
School year										
year 7	0	1	0	0	1	1	0	1	1	*312*
year 8	2	2	2	0	4	3	3	3	4	*266*
year 9	7	9	6	5	10	10	7	10	13	*284*
year 10	15	24	18	13	15	17	21	23	24	*285*
year 11	28	28	30	23	27	25	24	30	34	*262*

Table 2.4 Smoking behaviour by region: 1982 to 1996

All pupils   *England*

Region	1982	1984	1986	1988	1990	1992	1993	1994	1996
Regular smokers (%)									
North	11	11	9	8	10	12	9	10	15
Midlands/Wales*	8	13	10	6	10	5	11	13	13
South	13	15	10	9	10	10	9	12	10
Greater London	11	14	10	10	9	10	8	11	13
Occasional smokers (%)									
North	6	7	5	4	6	6	7	9	8
Midlands/Wales*	7	8	4	4	4	7	7	8	8
South	11	11	6	6	8	7	8	10	10
Greater London	5	7	7	7	7	8	11	9	8
Used to smoke (%)									
North	10	11	9	10	7	7	10	6	10
Midlands/Wales*	8	9	11	8	7	6	8	10	8
South	12	11	11	8	6	7	7	8	8
Greater London	13	11	8	6	9	4	7	6	6
Tried smoking once (%)									
North	23	23	20	19	20	20	21	22	20
Midlands/Wales*	23	24	22	20	20	20	17	15	18
South	25	24	21	21	19	21	22	19	20
Greater London	23	22	19	27	24	22	21	20	22
Has never smoked (%)									
North	50	49	57	60	57	55	53	52	48
Midlands/Wales*	53	46	53	62	59	63	57	54	53
South	38	39	52	57	56	56	54	52	51
Greater London	48	45	56	50	52	56	53	53	51
Bases (=100%)									
North	*966*	*1092*	*910*	*929*	*1072*	*1020*	*871*	*939*	*885*
*Midlands/Wales**	*834*	*1061*	*910*	*772*	*805*	*807*	*856*	*670*	*732*
South	*932*	*1114*	*1034*	*991*	*988*	*1102*	*1094*	*1075*	*890*
Greater London	*247*	*389*	*338*	*354*	*256*	*366*	*319*	*361*	*347*

* Wales was part of the England and Wales sample in 1982, 1984 and 1986
From 1988 onwards, figures are for the Midlands only

Table 2.5 Number of cigarettes smoked in the previous seven days, by sex

Current smokers *England 1996*

Cigarette consumption	Boys	Girls	Total
Regular smokers (%)			
None	3	2	3
1-5	7	5	6
6-10	6	9	7
11-20	15	12	13
21-70	45	49	45
71 or more	25	23	25
Mean	56	47	51
Median	46	40	44
Occasional smokers (%)			
None	16	23	20
1-5	50	55	53
6-10	12	12	12
11-20	12	5	8
21-70	7	4	5
71 or more	2	1	2
Mean	8	5	7
Median	3	2	2
All smokers (%)			
None	8	11	10
1-5	25	25	25
6-10	8	10	9
11-20	14	9	11
21-70	27	31	29
71 or more	18	14	16
Mean	36	30	33
Median	18	15	16
Base(=100%)			
Regular smokers	*154*	*208*	*362*
Occasional smokers	*107*	*141*	*248*
All smokers	*261*	*349*	*610*

Table 2.6   Mean and median cigarette consumption in the diary week by sex: 1982 to 1996
All pupils   *England*

	1982	1984	1986	1988	1990	1992	1993	1994	1996
Boys									
Regular smokers									
Mean	50	49	53	52	56	58	51	54	56
Median	40	40	43	49	48	51	40	44	46
Occasional smokers									
Mean	7	5	5	7	7	6	6	7	8
Median	2	1	1	3	3	1	2	2	3
Mean consumption per pupil	6	7	4	4	6	5	5	6	7
Girls									
Regular smokers									
Mean	44	49	45	41	49	44	44	47	47
Median	36	38	36	38	40	34	34	37	40
Occasional smokers									
Mean	4	4	4	4	4	3	4	3	5
Median	1	2	1	1	2	1	1	2	2
Mean consumption per pupil	5	7	6	4	5	4	5	6	8
Total									
Regular smokers									
Mean	47	49	48	46	53	51	47	50	51
Median	38	39	38	41	43	42	36	39	44
Occasional smokers									
Mean	6	4	5	6	6	5	5	5	7
Median	1	1	1	1	2	1	1	2	2
Mean consumption per pupil	6	7	5	4	6	5	5	6	7
Bases (=100%)									
Boys									
Regular smokers	*166*	*251*	*123*	*107*	*148*	*134*	*131*	*147*	*154*
Occasional smokers	*106*	*168*	*88*	*70*	*98*	*96*	*110*	*138*	*107*
All pupils	*1460*	*1928*	*1676*	*1488*	*1640*	*1641*	*1610*	*1515*	*1442*
Girls									
Regular smokers	*159*	*221*	*183*	*136*	*158*	*147*	*163*	*200*	*208*
Occasional smokers	*130*	*152*	*82*	*76*	*90*	*96*	*130*	*143*	*141*
All pupils	*1514*	*1689*	*1508*	*1529*	*1478*	*1597*	*1523*	*1521*	*1408*
Total									
Regular smokers	*326*	*474*	*306*	*246*	*306*	*281*	*294*	*347*	*362*
Occasional smokers	*236*	*324*	*170*	*148*	*188*	*192*	*240*	*281*	*248*
All pupils	*2979*	*3658*	*3189*	*3017*	*3118*	*3245*	*3133*	*3036*	*2850*

Table 2.7 Length of time as a regular smoker, by sex: 1988 to 1996

Regular smokers *England*

Length of time as a regular smoker	1988	1990	1992	1994	1996
	%	%	%	%	%
Boys					
Less than 3 months	11	8	17	13	7
3-6 months	14	14	14	8	5
6 months to 1 year	21	16	12	19	19
More than 1 year	54	62	57	61	69
Base(=100%)	*106*	*146*	*143*	*150*	*150*
	%	%	%	%	%
Girls					
Less than 3 months	10	11	11	11	10
3-6 months	11	13	18	13	9
6 months to 1 year	21	23	14	22	16
More than 1 year	57	53	57	54	65
Base(=100%)	*134*	*153*	*162*	*195*	*198*
	%	%	%	%	%
Total					
Less than 3 months	11	9	14	12	9
3-6 months	13	14	16	11	7
6 months to 1 year	21	19	13	20	18
More than 1 year	55	58	57	57	67
Base(=100%)	*243*	*299*	*305*	*345*	*348*

Table 2.8 Whether regular smokers would find it easy or difficult (a) not to smoke for a week (b) to give up smoking altogether, by sex: 1994 and 1996

Regular smokers *England*

Difficulty or ease of:	1994 Boys	Girls	Total	1996 Boys	Girls	Total
	%	%	%	%	%	%
Not smoking for a week						
Very difficult	19 }54	24 }61	22 }58	33 }66	31 }64	32 }65
Fairly difficult	34	37	36	33	33	33
Fairly easy	30 }46	27 }39	28 }42	24 }34	26 }36	25 }35
Very easy	16	12	14	10	10	10
	%	%	%	%	%	%
Giving up altogether						
Very difficult	30 }66	38 }73	35 }70	43 }76	44 }75	44 }75
Fairly difficult	36	35	35	33	31	32
Fairly easy	22 }34	20 }27	21 }30	17 }24	21 }25	19 }25
Very easy	12	7	9	7	5	6
Base (=100%)	*148*	*195*	*343*	*150*	*199*	*349*

Table 2.9 Whether regular smokers (a) would like to give up smoking altogether (b) have ever tried to give up smoking by sex: 1994 and 1996

Regular smokers *England*

	1994 Boys	Girls	Total	1996 Boys	Girls	Total
	%	%	%	%	%	%
Would like to give up						
Yes	36	33	34	45	44	45
No	20	18	19	21	9	14
Don't know	44	49	47	33	47	41
	%	%	%	%	%	%
Have tried to give up						
Yes	52	70	62	67	80	75
No	48	30	38	33	20	25
Base (=100%)	*149*	*195*	*344*	*150*	*199*	*349*

Table 2.10 Whether regular smokers would like to give up by whether they have tried, by sex

Regular smokers *England 1996*

Whether would like to give up	Whether has ever tried to give up		
	Yes	No	Total
	%	%	%
Boys			
Yes	56	24	45
No	12	40	21
Don't know	32	36	33
	%	%	%
Girls			
Yes	52	13	44
No	7	18	9
Don't know	41	69	47
	%	%	%
Total			
Yes	53	19	45
No	9	30	14
Don't know	38	51	41
Base (=100%)			
Boys	*100*	*50*	*150*
Girls	*160*	*39*	*199*
Total	*260*	*89*	*349*

Table 2.11 Perceived dependency on smoking by sex and length of time as a regular smoker

Regular smokers *England 1996*

Dependency	Length of time as a smoker					
	Boys		**Girls**		**Total**	
	1 year or less	More than one year	1 year or less	More than one year	1 year or less	More than one year
Would find it difficult not to smoke for a week	47	75	42	76	44	75
Would find it difficult to give up altogether	62	83	55	85	58	84
Would like to give up altogether	47	45	41	46	43	45
Has tried to give up	51	74	67	88	60	81
Base (=100%)	*47*	*103*	*69*	*129*	*116*	*232*

Table 2.12 Mean number of cigarettes smoked in the previous seven days by sex and whether not smoking for a week would be easy or difficult

Regular smokers *England 1996*

Difficulty or ease of not smoking for a week	Boys	Girls	Total
	Mean number of cigarettes		
Difficult	72	60	65
Easy	24	23	23
All regular smokers	56	46	50
Bases (=100%)			
Difficult	*99*	*127*	*226*
Easy	*51*	*71*	*122*
All regular smokers	*150*	*198*	*348*

Table 2.13 Mean number of cigarettes smoked in the previous seven days by sex and whether it would be easy or difficult to give up smoking altogether

Regular smokers *England 1996*

Difficulty or ease of giving up smoking altogether	Boys	Girls	Total
	Mean number of cigarettes		
Difficult	64	54	58
Easy	29	23	26
All regular smokers	56	46	50
Bases (=100%)			
Difficult	*114*	*148*	*262*
Easy	*36*	*50*	*86*
All regular smokers	*150*	*198*	*348*

3 Where children get their cigarettes

3.1 Purchase of cigarettes

Although it is illegal for cigarettes to be sold to children under the age of 16, previous surveys in the series have shown that many children do successfully buy cigarettes over the counter. The Children and Young Persons (Protection from Tobacco) Act 1991 greatly increased the penalties for the sale of tobacco to persons under the age of 16. The Act also made it illegal for shopkeepers to sell unpackaged cigarettes and required warning statements to be displayed in all retail premises and on cigarette vending machines.

In 1996, a quarter of pupils, 25%, attempted to buy cigarettes from a shop. The proportion of pupils who attempted to purchase cigarettes from a shop has remained within two percentage points of this level throughout the series of surveys, apart from in 1990, when a figure of 32% was recorded. Unsurprisingly, since a higher proportion of girls smoked than boys, they were more likely to have tried to purchase cigarettes (28% compared with 22%).

As expected from their smoking behaviour, the proportion of children trying to buy cigarettes increased with age, with 5% of 11 year olds having attempted to buy cigarettes compared with 54% of 15 year olds.

The proportion of boys and girls who were refused at least once in the last year when attempting to buy cigarettes from a shop rose from 35% in 1994 to its highest level in this series of surveys, 38%, in 1996.

In 1996, a higher proportion of girls than boys were refused by shopkeepers (39% compared with 36%) although the difference was not statistically significant. This reverses the pattern shown in most previous surveys. Generally, younger children were more likely to be refused cigarettes than older children. For example, 47% of 12 year olds who had attempted to buy cigarettes were refused at least once compared with 33% of 15 year olds.

Figure 3.1, Tables 3.1-3.2

3.2 Last time children tried to buy cigarettes from a shop

As well as being asked if they had been refused cigarettes in a shop at any time in the last year, pupils were also asked what had happened the last time they tried to buy cigarettes.

Eleven per cent of pupils were refused the last time they tried to buy cigarettes in a shop. Not surprisingly, younger children were more likely to have been refused than older children - 35% of 11 and 12 year olds, but only 3% of 15 year olds were refused the last time they tried to buy cigarettes from a shop.

Current smokers were also less likely to have been refused on their last attempt to buy cigarettes than those who had never smoked - 6% of regular smokers were refused compared with 21% of those who had never smoked. This could partly be explained by the association between smoking behaviour and age; those who have

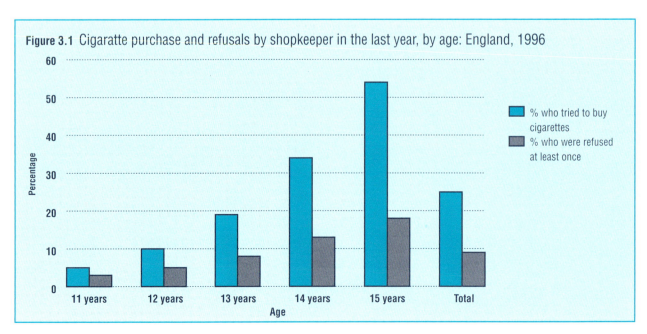

Figure 3.1 Cigaratte purchase and refusals by shopkeeper in the last year, by age: England, 1996

Legend:
- % who tried to buy cigarettes
- % who were refused at least once

never tried smoking tend to be younger, but it is also possible that smokers are more likely to know which shops will sell them cigarettes and which shops are likely to refuse them.

Tables 3.3-3.4

3.3 Who were the cigarettes bought for

The last time children purchased cigarettes in a shop, over half (53%) were buying them for themselves; a third (33%) said they were buying them for a friend, while 7% said they were buying them for their mothers and 3% for their fathers.

Of those children who had bought cigarettes the last time they tried, older children and current smokers were more likely to have bought cigarettes for themselves, whereas younger children and non-smokers were more likely to have purchased cigarettes for their parents. For example, 59% of 15 year-olds bought cigarettes for themselves compared with only 24% of 11/12 year-olds, and 1% of regular smokers bought cigarettes for their mothers compared with 29% of those who had never smoked.

Tables 3.3-3.4

3.4 Perceived difficulty of buying cigarettes from a shop

In 1996, those who smoked were asked for the first time to rate how difficult or easy they found it to buy cigarettes from a shop. Of those who bought cigarettes from a shop, only 15% of girls and 22% of boys said they found it difficult. Occasional smokers were more likely than regular smokers to perceive purchasing cigarettes from a shop as difficult (28% compared with 15%).

Unsurprisingly, a higher proportion of those who had been refused by a shopkeeper said they found it difficult to purchase cigarettes compared with those who had not been refused (17% compared with 6%). Interestingly, 83% of those who had been refused by a shopkeeper still felt that it was easy to buy cigarettes from a shop.

Tables 3.5- 3.6

3.5 How many cigarettes were bought last time

The last time pupils purchased cigarettes in a shop, almost half (49%) bought them in packs of

ten. Younger pupils were more likely than older children to buy cigarettes singly, 9% of those aged 11/12 had done so, compared with only 1% of those aged 15, although this difference was not statistically significant.

The proportion of pupils who purchased cigarettes in packs of ten the last time they bought some has been increasing over the series of surveys from 38% in 1988 to 49% in 1996, whilst the proportion of pupils who had purchased cigarettes in packets of 20 has been decreasing.

Figure 3.2, Tables 3.7-3.9

3.6 How current smokers obtain their cigarettes

Pupils who were current smokers were asked where they usually got their cigarettes from. If they often got cigarettes from different sources they were asked to tick more than one box.

Most smokers bought their cigarettes from shops, with newsagents or tobacconists (69%) and garage shops (41%) being the most common sources. Fifty-nine per cent of current smokers regularly obtained cigarettes from their friends while a quarter regularly bought cigarettes from a machine.

Younger smokers were most likely to have obtained their cigarettes from friends (61% of 13 year-olds) while older smokers were most likely to have bought their cigarettes from newsagents or tobacconists (70% of those aged 14 and 84% of those aged 15).

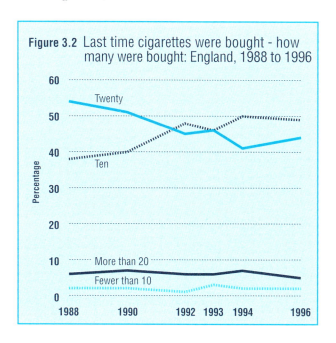

Figure 3.2 Last time cigarettes were bought - how many were bought: England, 1988 to 1996

Regular smokers were more likely than occasional smokers to have bought their cigarettes from a shop or machine, whereas occasional smokers were more likely to be given cigarettes by friends. This difference may reflect the fact that regular smokers tend to be older than occasional smokers and find it easier to buy cigarettes, as well as their knowing which shops are likely to sell them cigarettes. Regular smokers were twice as likely as occasional smokers to have been given cigarettes by their siblings (16% of regular smokers compared with 8% of occasional smokers) and more than three times as likely to have been given them by their parents (7% compared with 2%).

Figure 3.3, Table 3.10-3.11

Comparing with the last survey's results, a similar proportion of regular smokers obtained cigarettes from each source as in 1994.

Table 3.12

3.7 Financing the purchase of cigarettes

The amount of money pupils said they had to spend each week increased with age from an average of £3.81 per week for 11 year olds to £11.05 per week for 15 year olds. Twenty-two per cent of 11 year olds had either no spending money or less than £1 per week, compared with only 4% of 15 year olds.

Current smokers of all ages had on average more spending money than pupils in general. Regular smokers had an average of £11.22 a week to spend as they liked, compared with occasional smokers who had an average of £7.98, and an average for all pupils of £7.15.

Tables 3.13-3.14

Ninety-two per cent of all pupils had some money to spend each week as they liked. This spending money came from a number of sources. Among children who had weekly spending money 85% received pocket money and 25% did paid work. Not surprisingly the proportion of pupils with spending money from paid work rose with age, from 10% of 11 to 12 year olds to 44% of 15 year olds.

Current smokers were almost twice as likely as non-smokers to have paid work (39% of smokers compared with 20% of non-smokers). Smokers were also more likely than non-smokers to have spending money from a source other than pocket money or paid work.

Table 3.15

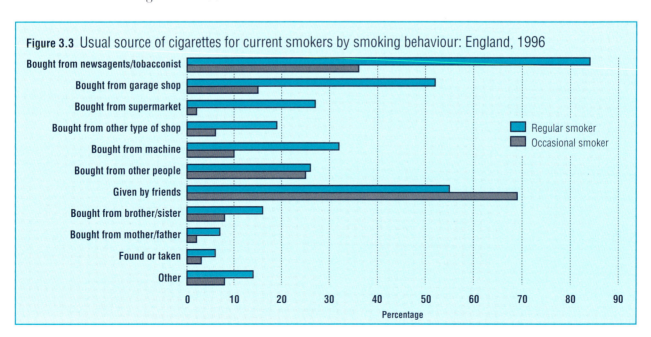

Figure 3.3 Usual source of cigarettes for current smokers by smoking behaviour: England, 1996

Regular smoker
Occasional smoker

Bought from newsagents/tobacconist
Bought from garage shop
Bought from supermarket
Bought from other type of shop
Bought from machine
Bought from other people
Given by friends
Bought from brother/sister
Bought from mother/father
Found or taken
Other

Percentage

Table 3.1 Cigarette purchase in the last year, by sex :
1986 to 1996

All pupils   *England*

	Boys	Girls	Total
% who tried to buy cigarettes			
1986	25	30	27
1988	26	27	26
1990	30	33	32
1992	25	25	25
1993	21	27	24
1994	24	29	26
1996	22	28	25
Was refused at least once :			
as % of those who tried to buy them			
1986	34	28	31
1988	30	26	27
1990	40	34	37
1992	36	36	36
1993	35	25	29
1994	39	32	35
1996	36	39	38
as % of all pupils			
1986	8	9	8
1988	8	7	7
1990	12	11	12
1992	9	9	9
1993	7	7	7
1994	9	9	9
1996	8	11	9
Bases (=100%)			
Those who tried to buy cigarettes			
1986	*409*	*454*	*865*
1988	*376*	*403*	*786*
1990	*488*	*483*	*971*
1992	*412*	*399*	*811*
1993	*337*	*407*	*744*
1994	*364*	*434*	*798*
1996	*322*	*384*	*706*
All pupils			
1986	*1757*	*1495*	*3157*
1988	*1469*	*1521*	*3016*
1990	*1627*	*1465*	*3092*
1992	*1657*	*1610*	*3267*
1993	*1602*	*1521*	*3123*
1994	*1516*	*1517*	*3033*
1996	*1443*	*1407*	*2850*

Table 3.2 Cigarette purchase in the last year, by age : 1986 to 1996

All pupils *England*

	11 years	12 years	13 years	14 years	15 years	Total
% who tried to buy cigarettes						
1986	16	15	21	30	45	27
1988	10	13	21	31	46	26
1990	18	18	27	39	54	32
1992	9	11	17	35	50	25
1993	5	10	17	32	50	24
1994	7	11	19	34	55	26
1996	5	10	19	34	54	25
Was refused at least once :						
as % of those who tried to buy them						
1986	41	47	39	30	22	31
1988	[47]	38	34	29	19	27
1990	46	52	44	31	29	36
1992	58	48	47	38	26	37
1993	[45]	48	30	36	21	29
1994	[54]	42	38	42	27	35
1996	[50]	47	42	39	33	38
as % of all pupils						
1986	7	7	8	9	10	8
1988	5	5	7	9	9	7
1990	8	9	12	12	16	12
1992	5	6	8	13	13	9
1993	2	5	5	11	10	7
1994	4	5	7	14	15	9
1996	3	5	8	13	18	9
Base (=100%)						
Those who tried to buy cigarettes						
1986	*74*	*96*	*128*	*198*	*369*	*865*
1988	*47*	*77*	*131*	*196*	*335*	*786*
1990	*105*	*110*	*158*	*234*	*360*	*971*
1992	*52*	*79*	*119*	*211*	*344*	*805*
1993	*24*	*62*	*111*	*207*	*333*	*737*
1994	*35*	*67*	*123*	*207*	*366*	*798*
1996	*28*	*57*	*104*	*200*	*317*	*706*
All pupils						
1986	*446*	*628*	*610*	*654*	*818*	*3157*
1988	*455*	*595*	*613*	*626*	*727*	*3016*
1990	*601*	*619*	*598*	*605*	*662*	*3092*
1992	*587*	*693*	*685*	*605*	*686*	*3256*
1993	*501*	*630*	*673*	*658*	*668*	*3130*
1994	*500*	*613*	*635*	*615*	*670*	*3033*
1996	*545*	*575*	*559*	*585*	*586*	*2850*

Table 3.3 Last time bought cigarettes - who the cigarettes were for, by age

All pupils who attempted to buy cigarettes in the last year *England 1996*

	11/12 years	13 years	14 years	15 years	Total
% who were successful last time	65	82	89	97	89
Who the cigarettes were for:*					
Self	24	52	52	59	53
Mother	20	7	6	5	7
Father	7	1	3	3	3
A friend	29	47	35	29	33
Brother or sister	4	4	3	2	3
Someone else	27	8	10	9	11
Bases(=100%)					
All who were successful last time	*55*	*85*	*178*	*306*	*624*
All who tried to buy in the last year	*84*	*104*	*200*	*317*	*705*

* Percentages total more than 100 because some pupils gave more than one answer.

Table 3.4 Last time bought cigarettes - who the cigarettes were for, by smoking behaviour

All pupils who attempted to buy cigarettes in the last year *England 1996*

	Regular smoker	Occasional smoker	Used to smoke	Tried once	Never smoked	Total
% who were successful last time	94	83	88	84	79	89
Who the cigarette were for :*						
Self	89	42	13	0	0	53
Mother	1	3	10	20	29	7
Father	1	2	0	9	15	3
A friend	16	44	65	56	33	33
Brother or sister	1	4	5	2	4	3
Someone else	4	13	13	18	35	11
Bases(=100%)						
All who were successful last time	*303*	*116*	*84*	*66*	*55*	*624*
All who tried to buy in the last year	*321*	*140*	*95*	*79*	*70*	*705*

* Percentages total more than 100 because some pupils gave more than one answer.

Table 3.5 Perceived difficulty or ease of buying cigarettes from a shop by sex, and smoking status

Smokers who had bought from shop *England 1996*

	Sex		Smoking status		Total
Difficulty or ease of buying cigarettes	Boys	Girls	Regular smoker	Occasional smoker	
	%	%	%	%	%
Difficult	22	15	15	28	18
Easy	78	85	85	72	82
Base (=100%)	*175*	*262*	*337*	*100*	*437*

Table 3.6 Perceived difficulty or ease of buying cigarettes from a shop by whether refused by shopkeeper in the last year

Smokers who had bought from shop *England 1996*

	Refused by shopkeeper		Total
Difficulty or ease of buying cigarettes	Yes	No	
	%	%	%
Difficult	17	6	12
Easy	83	94	88
Base (=100%)	*179*	*202*	*381*

Table 3.7 Last time cigarettes were bought - how many were bought by age

All pupils who had bought cigarettes *England 1996*

Cigarettes bought	11/12 years	13 years	14 years	15 years	Total
	%	%	%	%	%
Fewer than 10	9	5	1	1	2
Ten	43	53	48	49	49
Twenty	41	39	46	45	44
More than 20	7	4	5	4	5
Base (=100%)	*54*	*83*	*177*	*300*	*614*

Table 3.8 Last time cigarettes were bought - how many were bought by smoking behaviour

All pupils who had bought cigarettes *England 1996*

Cigarettes bought	Regular smoker	Occasional smoker	Used to smoke	Tried once	Never smoked	Total
	%	%	%	%	%	%
Fewer than 10	1	4	4	6	2	2
Ten	50	53	51	41	41	49
Twenty	44	41	38	52	54	44
More than 20	6	3	7	2	4	5
Base (=100%)	*300*	*114*	*82*	*64*	*54*	*614*

Table 3.9 Last time cigarettes were bought - how many were bought: 1988 to 1996

All pupils who had bought cigarettes *England 1996*

Cigarettes bought	1988	1990	1992	1993	1994	1996
	%	%	%	%	%	%
Fewer than 10	2	2	1	3	2	2
Ten	38	40	48	46	50	49
Twenty	54	51	45	46	41	44
More than 20	6	7	6	6	7	5
Base (=100%)	*693*	*809*	*680*	*642*	*686*	*614*

Table 3.10 Usual source of cigarettes for current smokers by smoking behaviour

Current smokers *England 1996*

Usual source of cigarettes*	Regular smokers	Occasional smokers	All current smokers
	Percentage from each source		
Bought from newsagents/ tobacconist/sweet shop	84	36	69
Bought from garage shop	52	15	41
Bought from supermarket	27	2	19
Bought from other type of shop	19	6	15
Bought from machine	32	10	25
Bought from other people	26	25	25
Given by friends	55	69	59
Given by brother/sister	16	8	13
Given by mother/father	7	2	5
Found or taken	6	3	5
Other	14	8	12
Bases(=100%)	*360*	*162*	*522*

*Percentages total more than 100 because many pupils gave more than one answer.

Table 3.11 Usual source of cigarettes for current smokers by age

Current smokers *England 1996*

Usual source of cigarettes*	11/12 years	13 years	14 years	15 years	All current smokers
	Percentage from each source				
Bought from newsagents/ tobacconist/sweet shop	[30]	47	70	84	69
Bought from garage shop	[13]	27	38	53	41
Bought from supermarket	[4]	7	14	30	19
Bought from other type of shop	[7]	10	14	18	15
Bought from machine	[26]	17	25	29	25
Bought from other people	[33]	30	34	17	25
Given by friends	[54]	61	60	59	59
Given by brother/sister	[9]	11	14	14	13
Given by mother/father	[2]	3	7	5	5
Found or taken	[4]	6	7	5	5
Other	[33]	17	14	6	12
Bases(=100%)	*46*	*88*	*152*	*236*	*522*

*Percentages total more than 100 because many pupils gave more than one answer.

Table 3.12 Usual source of cigarettes for regular smokers: 1982 to 1996

Regular smokers *England*

Usual source of cigarettes*	1982	1984	1986	1990	1992	1993	1994	1996
	Percentage from each source							
Bought from shop†	88	86	89	86	86	88	86	89
Bought from machine	13	20	19	37	27	35	31	32
Bought from other people	6	12	11	18	21	21	23	26
Given by friends	44	46	39	58	62	57	61	55
Given by brother/sister	9	7	12	19	16	16	18	16
Given by mother/father	10	7	7	5	7	8	7	7
Found or taken	1	1	2	3	4	6	6	6
Other	1	3	2	8	6	7	11	14
Base (=100%)	*325*	*474*	*300*	*305*	*310*	*297*	*348*	*360*

* Percentages total more than 100 because many pupils gave more than one answer.
† Prior to 1990 there was only one category for shop, as opposed to four post 1990.
For comparability since 1990, all the shop categories have been collapsed into one code.

Table 3.13 Amount of money pupils have to spend each week by age

All pupils *England 1996*

Weekly amount	11 years	12 years	13 years	14 years	15 years	Total
	%	%	%	%	%	%
Nothing	15	10	7	6	3	8
Less than £1 a week	7	5	2	1	1	3
£1 or more but less than £5	56	51	36	22	16	36
£5 or more but less than £10	17	26	38	41	35	31
£10 or more but less than £20	4	7	14	22	30	16
£20 or more a week	1	3	3	8	16	6
Mean amount (£) of spending money	3.81	5.07	6.71	8.78	11.05	7.15
Base(=100%)	*540*	*567*	*553*	*585*	*585*	*2830*

Table 3.14 Amount of money current smokers have to spend each week by age

Current smokers *England 1996*

Weekly amount	11/12 years	13 years	14 years	15 years	Total
	%	%	%	%	%
Nothing	5	2	6	2	3
Less than £1 a week	5	3	1	0	2
£1 or more but less than £5	45	26	19	12	20
£5 or more but less than £10	28	45	41	34	37
£10 or more but less than £20	12	21	22	34	25
£20 or more a week	4	4	12	18	12
Base(=100%)	*74*	*111*	*175*	*252*	*612*
Mean amount (£) of spending money					
All current smokers	6.23	8.09	9.57	12.00	9.90
Regular smokers	*	8.93	10.53	12.83	11.22
Occasional smokers	5.78	7.31	8.02	10.00	7.98
All pupils	4.45	6.71	8.78	11.05	7.15
Bases (=100%)					
All current smokers	*74*	*111*	*175*	*252*	*612*
Regular smokers	*22*	*54*	*108*	*178*	*362*
Occasional smokers	*52*	*57*	*67*	*74*	*250*
All pupils	*1107*	*553*	*585*	*585*	*2830*

* Base too small to allow reliable analysis

Table 3.15 Source of money pupils have to spend each week by age and smoking behaviour

All pupils with weekly spending money *England 1996*

Source *	11/12 years	13 years	14 years	15 years	Total
	%	%	%	%	%
Current smoker					
Pocket money	78	82	78	70	75
Paid work	16	34	36	50	39
Other	16	19	18	17	18
Non-smoker					
Pocket money	92	89	87	79	88
Paid work	9	20	31	39	20
Other	15	13	12	11	13
All pupils					
Pocket money	91	87	84	75	85
Paid work	10	23	32	44	25
Other	15	14	14	14	14
Base(=100%)					
Current smokers	*68*	*108*	*165*	*246*	*587*
Non-smokers	*881*	*403*	*385*	*316*	*1985*
All pupils with spending money	*949*	*511*	*550*	*562*	*2572*

* Percentages total more than 100 because some pupils could have more than one source.

4 The role of family and friends

Many previous studies have established that the development of children's smoking experience is influenced by the smoking behaviour of family and friends.[1-6] This chapter examines two particular aspects of this influence - the example set by family and friends in terms of their smoking behaviour, and related to this, the extent to which children grow up in an environment in which smoking is seen as acceptable.

The questions about parental and siblings' smoking behaviour, which have been included on the survey since 1984, were restructured in 1996 to make them easier for pupils to complete.

The parental smoking questions were separated into four individual questions. The pupils were asked whether they lived with their mother. This question had the written instruction "You should also answer 'Yes' if you live with your stepmother or adopted mother." (In previous years, this instruction was given to the pupils by the interviewer.) Those pupils who answered that they lived with their mother were routed to a question asking whether their mother smoked. The same pattern of questions was repeated for fathers' smoking behaviour. In past years, some pupils had difficulty in knowing how to record their answer, particularly when they were not living with both parents, and so left the question blank. This made it difficult to estimate with any great certainty the proportion of children living in homes where neither parent smoked. In 1996, the number of missing answers at these questions was a quarter of the number there had been in 1994. This suggests that the pupils found the new questions easier to follow.

The siblings' smoking behaviour questions were also altered in 1996 in order to collect more detailed information. The format of the grid-style questions can be seen in Appendix C. The revised 1996 question collected information on the number of siblings who smoked, as well as whether any did.

It must be remembered when looking at the trend data in tables 4.1, and 4.3 that the information in 1996 was collected using different questions.

4.1 Smoking in the pupil's family

In 1996, 30% of pupils lived with mothers who smoked and 29% lived with fathers who did. There was an increase in the proportion living with mothers who smoked between 1994 and 1996 but this may be due to the change to the question. There has been a significant decline in the level of parental smoking since 1984, when 37% said their mothers smoked and 44% said that their fathers smoked.

These figures are consistent with the General Household Survey (GHS), which has shown a decline among adults over the same period. The GHS does not provide figures for smoking among parents, but the age group that approximates most closely to this population is that aged 35-49. In the 1994 GHS, 31% of men and 28% of women in this age-group were current smokers in Great Britain.[7] Similarly on the 1995 Health Survey for England, 31% of men and 27% of women aged 35-44 were smokers.[8]

In 1996, 12% of pupils lived with at least one brother who smoked compared with 9% who lived with a sister who smoked. The increase in the proportion of pupils who lived with a brother who smoked from 7% in 1994 to 12% in 1996 may result from the question change in 1996.

Table 4.1

4.2 The influence of parental smoking

Pupils who lived with two parents who smoked were more than twice as likely to smoke as were those who lived in households where neither parent smoked (21% compared with 8%).

Among those pupils living with both parents, 11% of those who said that only their mother smoked were regular smokers themselves. This was a decrease compared with the 1994 figure of 20% but was more consistent with the level prior to 1994. For those who lived with two parents who both smoked, there was an increase in the proportion of pupils smoking regularly from 15% to 21% between 1994 and 1996. This increase may have resulted from the change in the question design.

Girls living with both parents were almost three times as likely as boys to be regular smokers if only their mother smoked (17% compared with 6%).

Among those children who said both their parents smoked, 57% said that they had tried smoking, compared with 41% of those with non-smoking parents. There was also a significant difference between boys and girls in families where only the mother smoked: 46% of boys had tried smoking but 60% of girls had done so.

As with children living with both parents, those in lone parent families were more likely to be regular smokers if that parent smoked than otherwise, although the difference was not statistically significant. Of those children who lived with a lone parent who smoked, 20% were regular smokers, compared with 13% of those who lived with a non-smoking lone parent.

Overall, 17% of those children who lived with a lone parent were regular smokers, compared with 12% of those who lived with both parents.

Tables 4.2-4.4

4.3 **The influence of sibling smoking**

The new format of the sibling smoking questions was designed to collect more detailed information than in the past. The two questions asking about brothers and then sisters used in 1994 were replaced by eight questions in 1996, which split older and younger brothers and sisters. However, this change led to more missing answers overall because some of the children, particularly the younger ones, had difficulty completing the more complicated layout. The new questions also incorporated separate answer categories for coding siblings' smoking behaviour as "Number I'm not sure about", which meant that more precise information was collected. A category 'Can't be sure whether any brothers/sisters smoke' was added to the tables to include those who were not sure about their siblings' smoking behaviour and those who had left the questions blank. This new group contained one fifth of the pupils.

Although parental smoking undoubtedly has a bearing on whether children become smokers or not, it has been shown in previous surveys that the influence of siblings is even more marked. In 1996, 30% of pupils who said they had a brother or sister who smoked were regular smokers, compared with only 7% of pupils who said that none of their brothers or sisters smoked. These figures are

similar to those for 1994 despite the change in the question format. Thirteen per cent of those who had no siblings (or those whose siblings did not live at home) were regular smokers, which suggests that the presence of non-smoking siblings at home may actually reduce the likelihood of a pupil being a smoker or, at least, delay the onset of experimentation with smoking. Ten per cent of those whose siblings' smoking behaviour could not be classified were regular smokers. As discussed earlier, these pupils were more likely to be younger and so their smoking prevalence is more likely to be associated with their age than the effect of siblings' smoking behaviour.

The pattern shown among regular smokers was also apparent in the proportions of children who had ever smoked, suggesting that the presence or absence of siblings who smoked also influences the extent to which children experiment with smoking. Girls were more likely to smoke regularly if they had no brother or sisters living at home than were boys (19% of girls compared with 7% of boys).

Girls with older brothers or sisters who smoked were more likely than boys with older siblings to smoke, although these differences were not statistically significant. For example, 34% of girls compared with 25% of boys with a smoking older sister were smokers. The small number of pupils with younger siblings who smoked prevents comparisons between this group and those with older siblings who smoked.

Figure 4.1, Table 4.5

The influence of siblings appears to decline as pupils get older. Among 11-12 year olds, those who said that they had brothers or sisters who smoked were twice as likely to have tried smoking (52%), as were those whose brothers or sisters did not smoke (25%). However among 15 year olds, 84% of those with at least one brother or sister who smoked had tried smoking, compared with 61% of those who had no brothers or sisters who smoked - a much less marked difference. It has been suggested that the influence of siblings in encouraging smoking may be particularly important at a young age because few of the pupil's peers smoke. As pupils get older, the influence of peers becomes stronger and consequently the role of siblings declines.[9]

Table 4.6

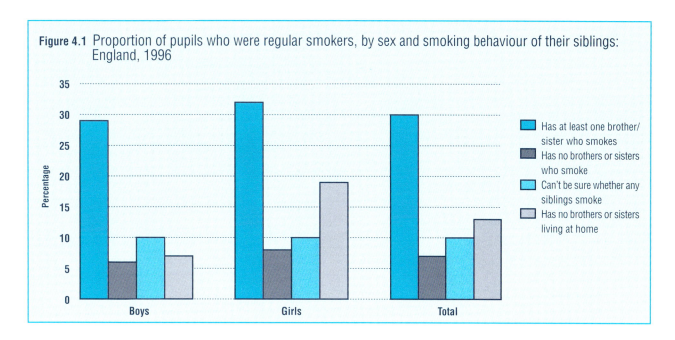

Figure 4.1 Proportion of pupils who were regular smokers, by sex and smoking behaviour of their siblings: England, 1996

Legend:
- Has at least one brother/sister who smokes
- Has no brothers or sisters who smoke
- Can't be sure whether any siblings smoke
- Has no brothers or sisters living at home

Pupils who had more than one sibling who smoked were no more likely to smoke than those with only one sibling who smoked - thirty-one per cent of those with two or more siblings who smoked were regular smokers compared with 27% of those with one sibling who smoked (this difference was not statistically significant).

Table 4.7

Although the smoking behaviour of siblings appears to have a greater influence on pupils' smoking experience than does the behaviour of their parents, the two factors are certainly related. However, examination of pupils' smoking behaviour in relation to both factors confirmed the finding from previous surveys that the influence of siblings is more powerful than that of parents. Those with brothers or sisters who smoked were at least four times more likely than pupils with non-smoking siblings to be smokers themselves, irrespective of the smoking behaviour of their parents. For example, in families where neither parent smoked, 26% of those with a sibling who smoked were regular smokers compared with 5% of those with non-smoking siblings.

Among those pupils with siblings who smoked, there was no clear pattern of variation in smoking behaviour according to whether or not their parents smoked. Among those with non-smoking siblings, the proportion of smokers was generally higher if parents smoked.

Table 4.8

4.4 The influence of friends' smoking

A further influence on pupils' smoking, particularly among older children, is likely to be the smoking behaviour of their friends. As in previous surveys, in 1996 there was a clear association between pupils' smoking behaviour and that of their friends. For example, 79% of regular smokers, but only 5% of pupils who had never smoked, said that all or most of their friends smoked.

Despite this clear association between pupils' smoking behaviour and that of their friends, it is not necessarily true that children smoke because their friends do. Peer influence has been shown to be strong, with children who smoke encouraging their friends into trying a cigarette. However, what has been called peer 'bonding' also exists[10] that those who smoke have more in common with each other and so tend to associate with each other. Studies have also suggested that non-smoking children can influence young smokers to become non-smokers.[11]

Table 4.9

4.5 Attitudes of the family towards pupils' smoking

Pupils were asked how their families felt (or would feel in the case of non-smokers) about their smoking. Current smokers were also given the opportunity to say that their family did not know they smoked. Although all these questions referred to the feelings of the family, it is likely that children were thinking primarily of their parents when they answered them.

The overwhelming majority of non-smokers thought that their families would disapprove of their smoking. Overall, 88% said that their parents would either try to stop them smoking or would persuade them not to, while only 1% said that their families would not mind if they smoked. Older non-smoking children were more likely than those who were younger to see their family's attitude as less authoritarian; the proportion who said their family would try to persuade them not to smoke rose with age, whereas the proportion who said they would stop them smoking fell.

Figure 4.2, Tables 4.10-4.11

Nearly a half of all current smokers (48%) thought that their families did not know they smoked. Previous surveys have consistently shown that girls were much more likely than boys to keep their smoking secret from their families. In 1996, the difference between girls and boys (49% compared with 45%) was not statistically significant. Occasional smokers were more likely than regular smokers to say that their families did not know they smoked: 68% did so, compared with 39% of regular smokers.

Regular smokers were three times as likely as occasional smokers to say their family would try to persuade them not to smoke (36% of regular smokers compared with 11% of occasional smokers).

Table 4.12

Parental smoking behaviour did not seem to have much effect on the attitude of pupils' families towards their smoking. Families in which neither parent smoked were only slightly more likely to be perceived as opposed to their child's smoking, than were families in which one or both parents smoked. Even in families where both parents smoked, 85% of non-smoking pupils said their parents would try and stop them smoking or persuade them not to smoke. Smokers were twice as likely to keep their smoking a secret if their parents did not smoke themselves than if both parents smoked - 63% of those with two non-smoking parents said their family did not know they smoked, compared with 31% of those where both parents smoked.

Table 4.13

Fourteen per cent of current smokers were allowed to smoke at home if they wanted to. In the 1994 survey, families appeared to be more tolerant of boys smoking than girls. However, in 1996, there was no significant difference in the proportion of boys and girls allowed to smoke at home (15% of boys and 13% of girls).

Table 4.14

References

1. Murray M, Swan AV, Johnson MRD and Bewley BR. Some factors associated with increased risk of smoking by children, *Journal of Child Psychology and Psychiatry*, 1983; 24, pp 223-32

2. Charlton A. The Brigantia smoking survey: a general review. *Public education about cancer.* UICC Technical Report Series, 1984; 77, pp 92-102

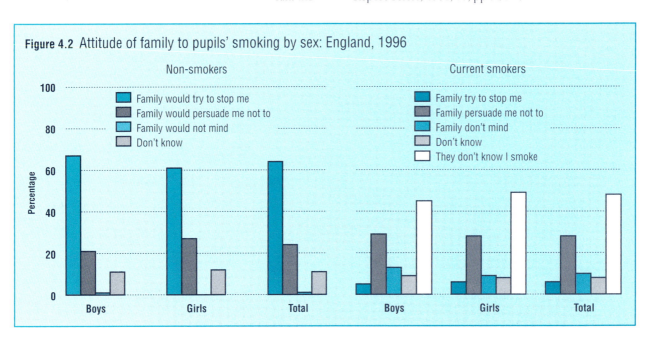

Figure 4.2 Attitude of family to pupils' smoking by sex: England, 1996

3. Murray M, Kiryluk S and Swan AV. Relation between parents' and children's smoking behaviour and attitudes, *Journal of Epidemiology and Community Health*, 1985; 39, pp 169-74

4. Nelson SC, Budd RJ, Eiser JR, Morgan M, Gammage P and Gray E. The Avon prevalence study: a survey of cigarette smoking in secondary schoolchildren, *Health Education Journal*, 1985; 44, pp 12-15

5. Charlton A and Blair V. Predicting the onset of smoking in boys and girls, *Social Science & Medicine*, 1989; 29, pp 813-18

6. Gillies PA and Galt M. Teenage smoking-fun or coping? in Winnbust JAM and Maes S (eds.) *Lifestyles and health: new developments in health psychology*, 1991; (Netherlands University Press)

7. Bennett N, Jarvis L, Rowlands O, Singleton N and Haselden L *Living in Britain: Results from the 1994 General Household Survey*, 1996 (London: HMSO)

8. Prescott-Clarke P and Primatesta P (eds.) *Health Survey for England 1995 Volume 1: Findings*, 1997 (London: The Stationery Office)

9. Goddard E *Why children start smoking*, 1990; (London: HMSO)

10. Royal College of Physicians Working Party. *Smoking and the young*, 1992 (London: Royal College of Physicians)

11. Banks MH, Bewley BR and Bland JM. Adolescent attitudes to smoking: their influence on behaviour, *International Journal of Health Education*, 1981; 24, pp 39-44

Table 4.1   Smoking behaviour of pupils' families: 1984 to 1996

All pupils   *England*

	1984	1988	1990	1992	1993	1994	1996	*Base(1996)* *=100%*
Mother smokes	37	32	33	28	26	27	30	*2816*
Father smokes	44	38	36	31	28	30	29	*2809*
At least one sister smokes	12	8	8	6	8	10	9	*2852*
At least one brother smokes	14	8	10	8	9	7	12	*2852*
Someone else in household smokes	5	9	10	8	7	7	10	*2818*

* Bases for earlier years are of a similar size and can be found in reports for each year

Table 4.2   Smoking behaviour of pupils, by sex and parental smoking behaviour

All pupils   *England 1996*

Parental smoking behaviour	Percentage who were regular smokers			Percentage who had ever smoked			*Bases (=100%)*		
	Boys	Girls	Total	Boys	Girls	Total	*Boys*	*Girls*	*Total*
Living with both parents (smoking and non-smoking)	10	14	12	45	50	47	*1148*	*1108*	*2256*
Neither parent smokes	7	9	8	40	42	41	*623*	*591*	*1214*
Only father smokes	14	16	15	52	56	54	*219*	*191*	*410*
Only mother smokes	6	17	11	46	60	53	*127*	*132*	*259*
Both parents smoke	18	25	21	52	61	57	*179*	*194*	*373*
Not living with both parents	14	19	17	60	57	58	*268*	*277*	*545*
No answer	[7]	[21]	13	[34]	[62]	47	*29*	*24*	*53*
Total	11	15	13	47	52	49	*1445*	*1409*	*2854*

Table 4.3 Smoking behaviour of pupils, by sex and parental smoking behaviour: 1988 to 1996

All pupils *England*

Parental smoking behaviour	Percentage who were regular smokers						Bases (=100%)					
	1988	1990	1992	1993	1994	1996	1988	1990	1992	1993	1994	1996
Boys												
Living with both parents												
Neither parent smokes	3	5	6	6	7	7	629	669	778	807	692	623
Only father smokes	4	8	8	9	9	14	167	225	211	170	172	219
Only mother smokes	7	14	8	8	16	6	94	110	106	100	90	127
Both parents smoke	14	13	15	14	10	18	268	318	247	211	208	179
Not living with both parents	16	12	16	12	18	14	123	176	194	194	241	268
No answer	9	13	7	8	8	[7]	208	145	126	131	119	29
Total	7	9	9	8	10	11	1489	1643	1662	1613	1522	1445
Girls												
Living with both parents												
Neither parent smokes	7	6	7	8	8	9	594	611	724	754	703	591
Only father smokes	7	9	8	9	10	16	233	202	208	147	183	191
Only mother smokes	8	11	11	12	23	17	107	104	120	100	112	132
Both parents smoke	11	17	14	15	21	25	261	270	247	185	213	194
Not living with both parents	11	16	17	17	20	19	132	168	216	242	220	277
No answer	11	15	10	9	11	[21]	202	123	111	99	92	24
Total	9	11	10	11	13	15	1529	1478	1626	1527	1523	1409
Total												
Living with both parents												
Neither parent smokes	5	6	6	7	7	8	1233	1280	1502	1561	1395	1214
Only father smokes	6	9	8	9	10	15	402	427	419	317	355	410
Only mother smokes	8	13	9	10	20	11	204	214	226	200	202	259
Both parents smoke	12	15	15	14	15	21	538	588	495	396	421	373
Not living with both parents	14	14	16	15	19	17	256	344	411	436	461	545
No answer	10	14	9	9	9	13	413	268	239	230	211	53
Total	8	10	10	10	12	13	3046	3121	3295	3140	3045	2854

Table 4.4 Smoking behaviour of pupils living with one parent only, by that parent's smoking behaviour

Pupils living with one parent only *England 1996*

	% who are regular smokers	% who have ever smoked	Bases (=100%)
Lives with:			
Smoking lone mother	18	63	213
Non-smoking lone mother	13	56	217
Smoking lone father	[28]	[75]	32
Non-smoking lone father	[14]	[50]	22
Smoking lone parent	20	64	245
Non-smoking lone parent	13	55	239
Total	17	60	484

Table 4.5 Smoking behaviour of pupils, by sex and the smoking behaviour of their siblings

All pupils *England 1996*

Siblings' smoking	Percentage who were regular smokers			Percentage who had ever smoked			Bases (=100%)		
	Boys	Girls	Total	Boys	Girls	Total	Boys	Girls	Total
Has at least one brother/sister who smokes	29	32	30	71	75	73	242	303	545
At least one older brother smokes	26	30	28	68	73	70	146	171	317
At least one older sister smokes	25	34	30	72	79	76	75	110	185
Only younger brother(s) or sister(s) smoke(s)	[62]	[36]	[49]	[86]	[77]	[81]	21	22	43
Has no brothers or sisters who smoke	6	8	7	38	40	39	740	663	1403
Can't be sure whether any brothers/sisters smoke	10	10	10	50	51	51	324	288	612
Has no brothers or sisters living at home	7	19	13	48	58	53	138	154	292
Total	11	15	13	47	52	49	1444	1408	2852

Table 4.6 Proportion of pupils who had ever smoked, by age and the smoking behaviour of their siblings
All pupils   *England 1996*

Siblings' smoking	11/12 years	13 years	14 years	15 years	Total
	Percentage who had ever smoked				
Has at least one brother or sister who smokes	52	68	87	84	73
Has no brothers or sisters who smoke	25	41	48	61	39
Can't be sure whether any brothers/sisters smoke	32	62	62	73	51
Has no brothers or sisters living at home	27	52	64	78	53
Total	30	52	62	72	49
Bases (=100%)					
Has at least one brother or sister who smokes	*143*	*116*	*134*	*152*	*545*
Has no brothers or sisters who smoke	*612*	*264*	*279*	*248*	*1403*
Can't be sure whether any brothers/sisters smoke	*271*	*119*	*112*	*110*	*612*
Has no brothers or sisters living at home	*94*	*61*	*61*	*76*	*292*
Total	*1120*	*560*	*586*	*586*	*2852*

Table 4.7 Smoking behaviour by number of siblings who smoke
Those with siblings who smoke   *England 1996*

	1 sibling smokes	2 or more siblings smoke
	%	%
Regular smokers	27	31
Occasional smokers	13	17
Used to smoke	13	10
Tried smoking	18	14
Never smoked	28	28
Base (=100%)	*332*	*125*

Table 4.8 Smoking behaviour of pupils, according to the smoking behaviour of their parents and their siblings
All pupils living with both parents   *England 1996*

Parental smoking behaviour	Siblings' smoking behaviour														
	Has at least one sibling who smokes	Has no siblings who smoke	Can't be sure whether any siblings smoke	Has no siblings living at home	Total	Has at least one sibling who smokes	Has no siblings who smoke	Can't be sure whether any siblings smoke	Has no siblings living at home	Total	*Has at least one sibling who smokes*	*Has no siblings who smoke*	*Can't be sure whether any siblings smoke*	*Has no siblings living at home*	*Total*
	Percentage who were regular smokers					Percentage who had ever smoked					*Bases (=100%)*				
Neither parent smokes	26	5	7	4	8	72	32	47	41	41	*148*	*713*	*258*	*95*	*1214*
Only father smokes	35	9	10	[13]	15	81	45	51	[46]	54	*85*	*205*	*81*	*39*	*410*
Only mother smokes	25	6	2	[19]	11	59	47	54	[67]	53	*63*	*129*	*46*	*21*	*259*
Both parents smoke	39	10	17	[18]	21	75	41	53	[62]	57	*118*	*133*	*83*	*39*	*373*
All living with both parents	32	6	9	10	12	73	37	50	49	47	*414*	*1180*	*468*	*194*	*2256*

Table 4.9 How many of pupil's friends smoke by smoking behaviour

All pupils   *England 1996*

Friends' smoking	Own smoking					
	Regular smoker	Occasional smoker	Used to smoke	Tried once	Never smoked	Total
	%	%	%	%	%	%
Boys						
All or most smoke	81	32	18	11	5	17
About half smoke	13	28	21	14	6	11
Only a few smoke	6	32	48	46	32	33
None smoke	0	7	13	29	58	38
Base (=100%)	*153*	*109*	*107*	*309*	*757*	*1435*
Girls						
All or most smoke	78	43	34	13	5	24
About half smoke	15	26	27	15	7	13
Only a few smoke	7	30	33	47	32	31
None smoke	0	1	6	24	57	32
Base(=100%)	*208*	*141*	*127*	*249*	*676*	*1401*
Total						
All or most smoke	79	38	26	12	5	20
About half smoke	14	27	24	15	6	12
Only a few smoke	6	31	40	46	32	32
None smoke	0	4	9	27	57	35
Base (=100%)	*361*	*250*	*234*	*558*	*1433*	*2836*

Table 4.10 Attitude of family to pupil's smoking, by sex*

All pupils   *England 1996*

Attitude of family	Boys	Girls	Total
Non-smokers			
Family would:			
try to stop me	67	61	64
persuade me not to	21	27	24
not mind	1	0	1
Don't know	11	12	11
Base (=100%)	*1167*	*1054*	*2221*
Current smokers			
Family:			
try to stop me	5	6	6
persuade me not to	29	28	28
don't mind	13	9	10
Don't know	9	8	8
They don't know I smoke	45	49	48
Base (=100%)	*207*	*316*	*523*

* Excludes pupils who were classified as occasional smokers but who were self-reported non-smokers on the questionnaire

Table 4.11   Attitude of family to pupils' smoking, by age*

All pupils   *England 1996*

Attitude of family	Age 11 years	12 years	13 years	14 years	15 years	Total
Non-smokers Family would :						
try to stop me	70	68	66	62	50	64
persuade me not to	15	18	22	32	41	24
not mind	1	0	0	0	2	1
Don't know	14	14	12	6	8	11
Base(=100%)	*515*	*520*	*445*	*408*	*333*	*2221*
Current smokers Family:						
try to stop me	-	[9]	3	8	4	6
persuade me not to	-	[15]	26	24	34	28
don't mind	-	[3]	3	12	12	10
Don't know	-	[6]	13	10	6	8
They don't know I smoke	-	[67]	54	47	44	48
Base(=100%)	*13+*	*33*	*89*	*152*	*236*	*523*

* Excludes pupils who were classified as occasional smokers but who were self-reported non-smokers on the questionnaire
+ Base too small to show data

Table 4.12   Perceived attitude of family among current
smokers by sex and smoking behaviour*

Current smokers   *England 1996*

Attitude of family	Regular smokers	Occasional smokers	All smokers
	%	%	%
Boys Family:			
try to stop me	3	9	5
persuade me not to	36	9	29
don't mind	13	11	13
Don't know	8	9	9
They don't know I smoke	39	61	45
Girls Family:			
try to stop me	6	7	6
persuade me not to	35	12	28
don't mind	12	2	9
Don't know	8	8	8
They don't know I smoke	38	71	49
Total Family:			
try to stop me	5	7	6
persuade me not to	36	11	28
don't mind	13	5	10
Don't know	8	9	8
They don't know I smoke	39	68	48
Bases(=100%)			
Boys	*153*	*54*	*207*
Girls	*209*	*107*	*316*
Total	*362*	*161*	*523*

* Excludes pupils who were classified as occasional smokers but who were self-reported non-
smokers on the questionnaire

Table 4.13 Attitude of family to pupils' smoking, by parental smoking*

All pupils   *England 1996*

Attitude of family	Parental smoking			Not living with both	Not answered	Total
	Living with both					
	Neither smoke	One smokes	Both smoke			
	%	%	%	%	%	%
Non-smokers						
Family would :						
try to stop me	66	62	61	63	[66]	64
persuade me not to	25	25	24	20	[17]	24
not mind	0	1	1	1	[0]	1
Don't know	9	12	14	15	[17]	11
Base(=100%)	*1017*	*512*	*258*	*393*	*41*	*2221*
Current smokers						
Family:						
try to stop me	4	4	5	11	-	6
persuade me not to	21	32	41	22	-	28
don't mind	6	10	10	16	-	10
Don't know	6	6	12	9	-	8
They don't know I smoke	63	48	31	43	-	48
Base(=100%)	*156*	*126*	*99*	*133*	*9+*	*523*

*Excludes pupils who were classified as occasional smokers but who were self-reported non-smokers on the questionnaire
+ Base too small to show data

Table 4.14 Whether pupils are allowed to smoke at home, by sex

Current smokers   *England 1996*

Whether allowed to smoke at home	Boys	Girls	Total
	%	%	%
Yes	15	13	14
No	70	74	72
Don't know	15	13	14
Base (=100%)	*208*	*315*	*523*

5 Children's attitudes to smoking

In 1994, the twelve questions about pupils' attitudes towards cigarette smoking that had been included previously in this series of surveys in 1984, were asked again. This provided the opportunity to see if there had been any changes in attitudes in the ten year period. In addition, a statement 'smoking makes your clothes smell' was included in 1994. These attitude statements were included again in the 1996 survey.

Some of the attitude statements were concerned with the health risks of smoking, for example; 'smoking can cause heart disease' and 'other people's smoking can harm the health of non-smokers'. Others were concerned with some of the psychological benefits smoking may be thought to provide, particularly for adolescents, for example; 'smoking gives people confidence' and 'smoking helps people relax if they feel nervous'.

The statements can also be considered as putting smoking in either a positive or a negative light, and this is how they are grouped in the tables. Pupils were asked to tick a box alongside each of the thirteen statements to show whether they thought it was true or not.

Between 1984 and 1994, there was a general shift towards more negative attitudes, which was particularly marked for the statements regarding the risk of passive smoking. The findings in 1996 were very similar to the 1994 results. The statements attracting the highest proportion of 'true' responses were those giving the adverse consequences of smoking, and, in particular, the health risks. Five out of the seven negative statements were agreed with by more than 90% of pupils: for example, 98% and 97% respectively agreed that 'smoking causes lung cancer' and that 'if a woman smokes when she is pregnant, it can harm her unborn baby'.

As in 1994, pupils were much less likely to think that the statements relating to possible positive benefits of smoking were true. In fact, between 1994 and 1996, there was a slight shift to less agreement with the 'positive' statements. Sixty-four per cent of pupils in 1996 agreed that 'smoking helps people relax if they feel nervous' compared with 67% in 1994. The percentage who agreed that smokers stay slimmer than non-smokers fell from 24% to 21% and there was also a decrease in the proportion who agreed that 'smoking gives people confidence'.

The attitudes of boys and girls towards the adverse consequences of smoking were similar, on the whole, except that boys were more likely to agree that smoking makes people worse at sports (85% of boys compared with 75% of girls). Boys were also more likely than girls to agree with the possible benefits of smoking 'smoking helps people cope better with life' and 'smokers are more fun', which is perhaps unexpected, given that boys are less likely than girls to be smokers.

It might be expected that attitudes would vary according to the pupil's own smoking experience, but this was not the case where the harmful consequences of smoking were concerned: smokers were just as likely to admit to these as were non-smokers. Smokers were, however, more likely to think that all the perceived positive consequences of smoking were true, except 'smoking gives people confidence' where the difference was not statistically significant. The most marked difference was for the statement 'smoking helps people relax if they feel nervous', which 87% of regular smokers, compared with only 53% of those who had never smoked, agreed with.

It is interesting that, far from being accompanied by a reduction in smoking prevalence, the shift between 1994 and 1996 towards a more negative view of the likely benefits of smoking occurred in spite of a small increase in the proportion who were smokers, and it occurred among smokers as well as non-smokers. This is perhaps not as surprising as might first be thought: the report on an earlier survey[1] suggested that children of this age do not have developed views about the consequences of smoking which are consistent with their own behaviour.

Tables 5.1-5.2

Reference

1. Goddard E. *Why children start smoking*, 1990: (London: HMSO)

Table 5.1 Smoking attitudes by sex: 1994 and 1996

All pupils   *England*

Proportion of pupils reporting that the following statements were true:	1994			1996		
	Boys	Girls	Total	Boys	Girls	Total
	%	%	%	%	%	%
"Negative" effects of smoking						
Smoking can cause lung cancer	98	98	98	98	98	98
If a woman smokes when she is pregnant, it can harm her unborn child	95	96	96	96	97	97
Smoking makes your clothes smell	96	97	96	96	97	96
Other people's smoking can harm the health of non-smokers	93	95	94	93	93	93
Smoking can cause heart disease	92	93	92	92	93	93
Smokers get more coughs and colds than non-smokers	78	81	79	79	78	79
Smoking makes people worse at sports	83	73	78	85	75	80
"Positive" effects of smoking						
Smoking helps people relax if they feel nervous	67	67	67	65	63	64
Smokers stay slimmer than non-smokers	26	23	24	21	20	21
Smoking gives people confidence	23	21	22	20	17	19
Smoking is not really dangerous, it only harms people who smoke a lot	23	16	20	22	16	19
Smoking helps people cope better with life	14	11	12	14	11	13
Smokers are more fun than non-smokers	7	3	5	5	3	4
Base (=100%)	*1470*	*1483*	*2953*	*1412*	*1391*	*2803*

Table 5.2 Smoking attitudes by smoking behaviour: 1994 and 1996

All pupils   *England*

Proportion of pupils reporting that the following statements were true:	1994						1996					
	Regular smoker	Occasional smoker	Used to smoke	Tried smoking	Never smoked	Total	Regular smoker	Occasional smoker	Used to smoke	Tried smoking	Never smoked	Total
	%	%	%	%	%	%	%	%	%	%		
"Negative" effects of smoking												
Smoking can cause lung cancer	99	98	98	98	98	98	97	96	98	98	98	98
If a woman smokes when she is pregnant, it can harm her unborn child	95	94	94	96	96	96	95	96	97	96	97	97
Smoking makes your clothes smell	96	97	96	95	97	96	96	96	98	96	97	96
Other people's smoking can harm the health of non-smokers	93	91	92	93	95	94	93	92	92	93	93	93
Smoking can cause heart disease	93	91	92	92	93	92	91	91	91	92	93	93
Smokers get more coughs and colds than non-smokers	75	75	80	80	81	79	76	76	76	79	80	79
Smoking makes people worse at sports	79	77	81	81	76	78	81	79	84	84	78	80
"Positive" effects of smoking"												
Smoking helps people relax if they feel nervous	86	81	74	69	58	67	87	75	73	66	53	64
Smokers stay slimmer than non-smokers	29	29	27	26	22	24	27	22	25	22	18	21
Smoking gives people confidence	26	28	27	24	19	22	21	20	20	20	17	19
Smoking is not really dangerous, it only harms people who smoke a lot	21	26	17	21	18	20	21	29	18	22	15	19
Smoking helps people cope better with life	25	17	12	14	9	12	25	19	13	12	9	13
Smokers are more fun than non-smokers	12	10	5	4	3	5	9	7	4	3	2	4
Base(=100%)	*327*	*266*	*214*	*528*	*1500*	*2835*	*355*	*245*	*233*	*552*	*1418*	*2803*

6 The health education message

In 1989, the Health Education Authority (HEA) launched its five-year Teenage Smoking Campaign. This aimed to dissuade young people from taking up smoking and to encourage current smokers to stop. In 1996, the HEA co-ordinated a new campaign titled 'Respect' which had the same anti-smoking purpose as their earlier campaign. The last three surveys in this series have included a number of questions designed to see how aware pupils were of the health risks of smoking and from what sources they received these health messages. However, just as the role of cigarette advertising in encouraging young people to smoke is complex,[1] so is the impact of health education in discouraging them.

6.1 Parental discussion about the health effects of smoking

All pupils were asked if anyone in their family had discussed the effects of smoking or passive smoking on their health with them in the past year. (No attempt was made to define what was meant by a discussion or to find out whether it was initiated by the parents or the child.)

Overall, 57% of pupils said that someone in their family had discussed the effects of smoking on their health with them in the past year. Girls were slightly more likely than boys to have had these discussions (59% of girls compared with 55% of boys). Pupils who were regular smokers were more likely to have discussed the subject than non-smokers; 70% of regular smokers had discussed the effects of smoking on their health with their families compared with 56% of those who had never smoked.

A smaller proportion, 39%, of pupils said that someone in their family had discussed the effects of passive smoking on their health within the past year. There was no difference in the proportions of current smokers and non-smokers who had discussed passive smoking with their parents.

Table 6.1

Between 1994 and 1996, there was no significant change in the proportion of pupils who had discussed the effects of smoking on their health with their families. However, the proportion of pupils who had discussed the effects of passive smoking with their families decreased, from 44% in 1994 to 39% in 1996.

Table 6.2

6.2 Health education in schools

One of the main themes of the HEA's Teenage Smoking programme was the development of school-based activities, especially the development of information and materials that can be used by teachers in health education classes. The new 'Respect' campaign has taken a different approach, using advertisements in teenage magazines to interest children in applying for a smoking fact file. However, smoking education has remained as a topic to be covered as part of the National Curriculum in science.[2] It has also been identified as an important cross-curricular theme by the National Curriculum Council.[3] It is therefore important, despite the change in focus of the HEA co-ordinated campaign to find out the health education lessons that children recall having received in school.

The pupils were asked if they could remember having had health education classes in the last year on dental health, healthy eating, drugs, alcohol, AIDS, solvents or smoking - thus including smoking education in the context of other health education topics. These topics, which had been asked about in 1994, were supplemented in 1996 by asking about lessons on exercise and sports, risks of sunbathing and sunburn, sex education and safe sex, and specific drugs - heroin, crack and ecstasy.

The proportion of pupils who remembered receiving health education on smoking increased from 65% in 1994 to 69% in 1996. On previous surveys, a higher percentage of pupils remembered receiving lessons on smoking than any other topic, apart from healthy eating. In 1996, the new topics of sex education and exercise and sports were also recalled by over 60% of the pupils.

Between 1994 and 1996, there was an increase in the percentage of pupils who remembered receiving lessons on all the topics covered in 1994. In particular, the proportion recalling lessons on drugs rose to 64%, a similar level to that for smoking and there was also a large increase for lessons on alcohol from 45% in 1994 to 55% in 1996.

Table 6.3

Older pupils were more likely than younger pupils to have received lessons on most topics, particularly those related to drugs and AIDS. For example, 58% of year 11 pupils had attended lessons on ecstasy compared with 28% of year 7 pupils. It should be noted, however, that the pupils completed the questionnaires in the autumn of 1996. Thus, for most of the period referred to in the question, pupils were one school year lower than at the time of fieldwork - and most year 7 pupils would have been at primary school.

Sixty-three per cent of year 7 pupils had received lessons on smoking in 1996 compared with 46% in 1994. This was at a similar level to older pupils - 71% of year 9 pupils, and 70% of year 11 pupils recalled lessons on smoking.

Table 6.4

References

1. Goddard E. *Why children start smoking*, 1990 (London: HMSO)

2. Department of Education and Science and the Welsh Office. *Science in the National Curriculum*, 1989 (London: HMSO)

3. National Curriculum Council. *Curriculum Guidance 5: Health Education*, 1990

Table 6.1 Whether pupils had discussed with their families the effects of smoking on their health, by sex and smoking behaviour

All pupils *England 1996*

Smoking behaviour	Boys	Girls	Total	Bases(=100%) Boys	Girls	Total
	% who have had discussion with their parents					
Had discussed health effects of smoking						
Regular smoker	68	72	70	*152*	*209*	*361*
Occasional smoker	49	56	53	*110*	*140*	*250*
Used to smoke	56	56	56	*107*	*128*	*235*
Tried once	50	57	53	*310*	*247*	*557*
Never smoked	55	57	56	*759*	*681*	*1440*
All pupils	55	59	57	*1438*	*1405*	*2843*
Had discussed health effects of passive smoking						
Regular smoker	37	38	37	*153*	*208*	*361*
Occasional smoker	37	34	36	*110*	*140*	*250*
Used to smoke	36	35	36	*107*	*128*	*235*
Tried once	36	41	39	*310*	*249*	*559*
Never smoked	44	39	42	*758*	*681*	*1439*
All pupils	40	39	39	*1438*	*1406*	*2844*

Table 6.2 Whether pupils had discussed with their families the effects of smoking on their health, by sex and smoking behaviour: 1994 and 1996

All pupils *England*

Smoking behaviour	1994 Boys	Girls	Total	1996 Boys	Girls	Total
	% who have had discussion with their parents					
Had discussed health effects of smoking						
Regular smoker	62	68	66	68	72	70
All pupils	57	56	56	55	59	57
Bases (=100%)						
Regular smoker	*152*	*201*	*353*	*152*	*209*	*361*
All pupils	*1516*	*1511*	*3027*	*1438*	*1405*	*2843*
Had discussed health effects of passive smoking						
Regular smoker	43	42	43	37	38	37
All pupils	46	42	44	40	39	39
Bases(=100%)						
Regular smoker	*152*	*201*	*353*	*153*	*208*	*361*
All pupils	*1510*	*1515*	*3025*	*1438*	*1406*	*2844*

Table 6.3 Proportion of pupils who remembered receiving health education on various topics in the last year: 1986, 1988, 1993, 1994 and 1996

All pupils   *England*

Health education lessons	1986	1988	1993	1994	1996
	%	%	%	%	%
Smoking	42	52	62	65	69
Dental health	47	52	38	35	40
Healthy eating	60	74	69	69	75
Drugs+	35	38	55	57	64
Alcohol		36	48	45	55
AIDS*			37	33	37
Solvents**				33	41
Exercise/sports***					65
Sunbathing/sunburn risks***					25
Sex education/safe sex***					67
Heroin***					36
Crack***					34
Ecstasy***					41
Base(=100%)	*3189*	*2759*	*2971*	*2971*	*2705*

+ drugs and alcohol were a combined answer category in 1986
* not asked in 1986 or 1988
** not asked in 1986, 1988 or 1993
*** not asked in 1986, 1988, 1993 or 1994

Table 6.4 Proportion of pupils who remembered receiving health education on various topics in the last year by school year
All pupils   *England 1996*

| Health education lessons | School year | | | | | |
	Year 7	Year 8	Year 9	Year 10	Year 11	Total
	%	%	%	%	%	%
Smoking	63	68	71	76	70	69
Dental health	57	49	40	28	24	40
Healthy eating	81	74	76	77	66	75
Drugs	54	53	62	74	77	64
Alcohol	43	46	57	65	65	55
AIDS	18	20	31	50	66	37
Solvents	37	28	39	50	53	41
Exercise/sports	63	66	67	68	64	65
Sunbathing/sunburn risks	28	25	23	23	23	25
Sex education/safe sex	60	69	62	73	74	67
Heroin	28	22	35	46	47	36
Crack	26	22	33	43	45	34
Ecstasy	28	24	40	53	58	41
Bases(=100%)	*597*	*517*	*537*	*542*	*512*	*2705*

7 Social and educational factors

The General Household Survey has consistently shown a strong association for adults between smoking and socio-economic group. In 1994, for example, men in unskilled manual households were more than twice as likely to smoke as were men in professional households (39% compared with 18%). Similarly, 32% of women in semi-skilled and unskilled manual households were smokers compared with 13% of those living in professional households.[1] Given that other aspects of the child's family circumstances, such as whether the parents smoke, are associated with smoking behaviour, it would be interesting to investigate whether an association is also found with parental socio-economic group.

There have been no attempts in this series of surveys to collect information on parents' occupation from the children. It was thought that even if the children knew their parents' occupations, it was unlikely that they would be able to give enough details for an accurate classification of their parents' socio-economic group to be made.

However, it was felt that children would be more likely to be able to give information about the consumer durables in their home, the number of cars the family has, and that they might also be able to say whether their parents own or rent their home. These can be used as indicators of a family's socio-economic position: for example, 60% of professional households have a home computer, compared with 17% of unskilled manual households.[2] Questions on these topics were therefore included on an experimental basis in 1996.

Some questions about educational expectations were also included for the first time. The children were asked whether they expected to stay in full-time education after the end of year 11 (the fifth year). In addition, more detailed information on educational level was collected by asking the children whether they expected to sit GCSEs and if so, whether they expected to pass more than five at Grades A, B or C. The questions provide a rough guide to educational ability, which has been shown to be related to some extent to socio-economic group.[3] Similar questions were asked on 'Why Children Start Smoking'[4] and were found to be associated with smoking - those with higher expectations being comparatively less likely to take up smoking.

7.1 Consumer durables and cars

Table 7.1 shows the overall percentage of pupils who said their family has one or more cars, a home computer and a dishwasher. When these figures are compared with GHS figures for households containing children aged 11-15, it can be seen that some pupils tend to over-report - 45% of the pupils lived in families that had 2 or more cars compared with 35% of children aged 11-15 on the GHS; 60% of the pupils' families had home computers compared with 54% on the GHS and 43% of the children lived in households with a dishwasher compared with 31% of children aged 11-15 on the GHS. It is not clear why the children are over-reporting availability of consumer durables and cars, but this should be borne in mind when considering any association between availability of these items and smoking behaviour.

Table 7.1

Looking at the proportion of regular smokers according to consumer durables the family has, the only significant difference was found for home computers. Fifteen per cent of those who live in families that do not have a computer were regular smokers compared with 11% of those in households with home computers. Assuming that having a home computer indicates a higher socio-economic position, this is a similar association to that for adults noted earlier. However, among children, the same association was not found for car and dishwasher availability, which might also have been expected to indicate higher socio-economic group and therefore be associated with smoking prevalence.

When the sexes are looked at separately, the expected variation in prevalence according to car availability was found for girls - those whose families did not have a car were more likely to smoke than girls from families with cars (19% compared with 14%), although the difference was not statistically significant.

Table 7.2

As this is the first year that these questions have been asked it is difficult to determine whether or not the quality of the children's answers has affected which items are associated with higher smoking prevalence. From the comparison with the GHS data, it would appear that the data collected on availability of home computers was more accurately reported by the pupils, and this may be why an association was found only between this item and smoking. Alternatively, family ownership of some of the items asked about may not be associated with children's smoking behaviour.

7.2 Tenure

The proportion of owner occupier households reported by the pupils was the same as for GHS households containing children aged 11-15 - 71% on both surveys. However, since 12% of pupils on this survey did not know whether their home was owned or rented, this apparent agreement is misleading. If the "don't know's" are excluded, then pupils on this survey were more likely to say that their family owned their home than would be expected from the GHS. Pupils aged 11 were more than twice as likely as were those aged 15 not to know whether their home was owned or rented (16% compared with 7%). The 15 year olds may be more likely to guess whether their home was owned or rented if they did not know and if so, they were more likely to guess that their family were owner-occupiers.

Tables 7.3-7.4

Fifteen per cent of pupils who said their families rented were regular smokers compared with 12% of those whose families were owner occupiers (although the difference was not statistically significant). Boys were more likely to be regular smokers if their families rented rather than owned (15% compared with 9%). There was no significant difference for girls.

Table 7.5

On the whole, these data do not provide much evidence of an association between children's smoking and the socio-economic position of the family, although such pointers as there are suggest that if anything, those in less affluent households may be more likely to smoke than are other children. However, because of the lack of consistency in the data, these findings are only tentative at present. It may be that other factors such as parental smoking, which is related to both social factors and children's smoking, have a greater influence on the prevalence of children's smoking.

7.3 Expected educational attainment

When asked whether they thought they would stay in full-time education after year 11, a third of pupils (34%) did not know whether they would. Unsurprisingly, younger children were twice as likely to give this answer as older children (46% of 11 year-olds compared with 21% of 15 year-olds).

Pupils who thought they would not stay in full-time education after year 11 were twice as likely to be regular smokers as those who thought they would (22% compared with 11%). This difference was particularly marked for boys - 23% of those who did not expect to stay on were regular smokers compared with 9% of those who expected to stay on.

Tables 7.6 - 7.7

The two questions asking about GCSE results were grouped in the analysis to show expectation of GCSE results. Again, the results must be considered with caution because almost half the sample (47%) said that they did not know whether they would take GCSEs or pass five or more of them.

Pupils who thought they would take GCSEs but not get as many as five passes were nearly three times as likely to be regular smokers as those who thought they would pass at least five (29% compared with 11%). There was little difference in smoking prevalence among the other categories of expectations of GCSE results.

Tables 7.8 - 7.9

Although those who did not expect to stay on at school were more likely than those who did to be smokers, the highest prevalence was found, not among those who did not think they would be taking GCSEs, but among those who expected to sit them, but thought they would not do well.

References

1. Bennett N, Jarvis L, Rowlands O, Singleton N and Haselden L *Living in Britain: Results from the 1994 General Household Survey*, 1996 (London: HMSO)
2. Rowlands O, Singleton N, Maher J and Higgins V *Living in Britain: Results from the 1995 General Household Survey*, 1997 (London: The Stationery Office)
3. Courtenay G *England and Wales Youth Cohort Study, Report on Cohort 1 Sweep 1*, Sheffield Training Agency (1988)
4. Goddard E *Why children start smoking*, 1990 (London: HMSO)

Table 7.1 Proportion of pupils whose family has a car, a home computer or a dishwasher compared with GHS 1995 data for children aged 11-15 in England

All pupils   *England*

	% of pupils	GHS - % of children aged 11-15
Number of family cars		
Two or more	45	35
One	45	47
None	10	17
Base (=100%)	*2814*	*1329*
Whether family has a home computer		
Yes	60	54
No	40	46
Base (=100%)	*2806*	*1329*
Whether family has a dishwasher		
Yes	43	31
No	57	69
Base (=100%)	*2807*	*1329*

Table 7.2 Proportion of pupils who were regular smokers, by sex and whether pupil's family has a car, a home computer or a dishwasher

All pupils   *England 1996*

	Bases(=100%)					
	Boys	Girls	Total	Boys	Girls	Total
	Percentage who were regular smokers					
Number of family cars						
Two or more	11	14	13	664	609	1273
One	9	14	12	611	643	1254
None	10	19	14	143	144	287
Whether family has a home computer						
Yes	9	13	11	900	796	1696
No	12	17	15	512	598	1110
Whether family has a dishwasher						
Yes	11	14	13	637	566	1203
No	9	15	12	776	828	1604

Table 7.3 Tenure of pupil's family home compared with GHS 1995 data for children aged 11-15 in England

All pupils   *England*

	% of pupils	GHS - % of children aged 11-15
Whether family owns or rents where they live		
Owns	71	71
Rents	17	29
Don't know	12	-
Base (=100%)	*2814*	*1329*

Table 7.4 Tenure by age

All pupils   *England 1996*

	11 years	12 years	13 years	14 years	15 years	Total
	%	%	%	%	%	%
Whether family owns or rents where they live						
Owns	68	68	71	74	74	71
Rents	16	19	16	17	18	17
Don't know	16	13	13	9	7	12
Base (=100%)	*536*	*564*	*556*	*578*	*580*	*2814*

Table 7.5 Proportion of pupils who were regular smokers, by sex and tenure

All pupils *England 1996*

	Boys	Girls	Total
	Percentage who were regular smokers		
Whether family owns or rents where they live			
Owns	9	15	12
Rents	15	16	15
Don't know	8	15	12
Bases (=100%)			
Owns	*1013*	*988*	*2001*
Rents	*250*	*236*	*486*
Don't know	*156*	*171*	*327*

Table 7.6 Whether pupils think they will stay in full-time education after the end of year 11 by age

All pupils *England 1996*

	11 years	12 years	13 years	14 years	15 years	Total
	%	%	%	%	%	%
Whether staying in full-time education after year 11						
Staying on	47	50	54	64	68	57
Not staying on	8	9	8	7	10	8
Don't know	46	41	38	28	21	34
Base=(100%)	*531*	*557*	*552*	*579*	*582*	*2801*

Table 7.7 Proportion of pupils who were regular smokers, by sex and whether they think they will stay in full-time education after the end of year 11

All pupils *England 1996*

Whether staying in full-time education after year 11	Boys	Girls	Total
	Percentage who were regular smokers		
Staying on	9	14	11
Not staying on	23	19	22
Don't know	9	16	13
Bases (=100%)			
Staying on	*768*	*832*	*1600*
Not staying on	*155*	*83*	*238*
Don't know	*490*	*473*	*963*

Table 7.8 Expectation of GCSE results by sex

All pupils *England 1996*

Whether expects to take GCSEs before leaving school	Boys	Girls	Total
	%	%	%
Thinks will take GCSEs			
expects to pass 5 or more	47	43	45
does not expect to pass 5 or more	5	5	5
not sure about likely results	28	38	33
Thinks will not take GCSEs	4	2	3
Not sure if will take GCSEs	16	12	14
Base(=100%)	*1445*	*1409*	*2854*

Table 7.9 Proportion of pupils who were regular smokers, by sex and expectation of GCSE results

All pupils *England 1996*

				Bases(=100%)		
Whether expects to take GCSEs before leaving school	Boys	Girls	Total	*Boys*	*Girls*	*Total*
	Percentage who were regular smokers					
Thinks will take GCSEs						
expects to pass 5 or more	8	14	11	*673*	*604*	*1277*
does not expect to pass 5 or more	29	29	29	*78*	*77*	*155*
not sure about likely results	12	14	13	*407*	*533*	*940*
Thinks will not take GCSEs	12	[17]	13	*59*	*23*	*82*
Not sure if will take GCSEs	9	13	11	*228*	*172*	*400*

Appendices

Appendix A **The sample**

A sample was required of children of secondary school age with separate national samples for England and Scotland. The sample for Scotland is described in the separate report for Scotland.[1]

In England the target population was children who were in years 7 to 11 inclusive in secondary schools or at an equivalent level in middle and upper schools.

The survey covered almost all types of secondary school (comprehensive, secondary modern, grammar, technical, and other secondary schools) in both the maintained and non-maintained sectors of education. Only pupils attending special schools (for children with learning disabilities) and hospital special schools (for children spending a period in hospital) were excluded from the survey.

The sample was selected in two stages. At the first stage a sample of schools was selected from a list of all schools in England taken from the 1996 school database supplied by the School's Register for the Department for Education and Employment. At the second stage an interviewer visited each selected school and drew a sample of pupils from school registers.

Probabilities of selection

Given the requirement that each child in the target population should have the same probability of being selected to take part in the survey, the overall probability of selection, or sampling fraction, is the product of the sampling fractions at the first and second stages, i.e.

$$F = f_1 \times f_2$$

where f_1 = probability of selecting the school
f_2 = probability of selecting the pupil

Schools with probability proportional to the number of pupils aged 11-15, so that roughly equal numbers of pupils could be sampled from each selected school. Thus :

$$f_1 = n_1 \times \frac{s}{S}$$

where n_1 = total number of schools to be selected
s = number of pupils in an individual school aged 11-15
S = total number of pupils aged 11-15

and

$$f_2 = \frac{n_2}{S}$$

where n_2 = number of pupils to be selected from each school

Overall, therefore, for each pupil the sampling fraction is :

$$F = (n_1 \times \frac{s}{S}) \times (\frac{n_2}{s}) = \frac{n_1 \times n_2}{S}$$

Sample size

The survey aimed to achieve a sample of about 3,000 pupils in England. To achieve this a sample of 128 schools was drawn in England. Based on experience, it was expected that about 90% of schools would co-operate. Assuming that 90% of selected pupils would agree to take part in the survey, the average size of quota selected in each co-operating school to achieve the required sample size would be 30 pupils.

As in previous years, schools with fewer than 35 pupils in the required age ranges were deleted from the sampling frame.

Stratification of the sampling frame

Previous surveys in the series had shown that smoking behaviour varied according to the characteristics of the school rather more than it did by region, so schools were stratified in England as follows :

1. Into three school types :
    LEA maintained
    Grant maintained
    Independent

2. Then, by selection policy into:
    comprehensive
    selective
    secondary modern
(except for Independent schools which were separated into selective and non-selective)

3. Finally the larger strata were split into :
   boys only
   girls only
   mixed

4. In each of the 16 major strata formed, schools were ordered by local education authority within region.

Tables A1 shows the allocation of the required sample of schools to each of the major strata and the number of schools actually selected in England.

Table A1

Sampling within selected schools

Sampling fractions at the second stage (i.e. within schools) were calculated in the office and adjusted to compensate for the effect of rounding on the number of schools selected in each stratum at the first stage. Expected quota sizes are shown in Table A2. These were based on information about the number of pupils at each collected in the previous six months, and actual quota sizes therefore varied to the extent to which the size of the school had changed in the interim.

Table A2

Sampling at each co-operating school was carried out by an ONS interviewer. The instructions to which the interviewers worked were the same as in previous surveys.

Precision of results and the measurement of change

Since the data in this report were obtained from a sample of the population, they are subject to sampling error. Any sample is only one of an almost infinite number that might have been selected, all producing slightly different estimates. Sampling error stems from the probability that any selected sample is not completely representative of the population from which it is drawn.

Sampling error shows the amount by which the value of a sample estimate of a variable can be expected to differ from the true value of that variable in the population. With a simple random sample, the formula for calculating the sampling error for a percentage p, is :

$$\sqrt{\frac{p(100-p)}{n}}$$

where n is the sample size.

Since the sample of pupils was clustered in schools, the sampling errors are larger than they would have been for a simple random sample of the same size. Sampling errors for some key variables which take account of the complex design are shown later on in this chapter.

The formula for calculating sampling errors of differences in percentages between surveys assuming simple random samples is :

$$\sqrt{\frac{p_1(100-p_1)}{n_1} + \frac{p_2(100-p_2)}{n_2}}$$

In general, attention is drawn to differences between estimates only when they are significant at the 0.05 confidence level, thus indicating that there is less than a 5% probability that the observed difference is due to random sampling variation and that no difference occurred in the population from which the sample is drawn.

It is important to recognise that sampling error is only one of the sources of error which affect the accuracy of any survey results. Other sources of inaccuracy include non-response bias, and over- and under-reporting, both of which are difficult to quantify. It can be assumed, however, that since the results compared in this report are from surveys conducted in the same way and using the same methods of collecting information, non-sampling errors will be similar on each survey and so will not affect comparisons.

Sampling errors

Tables A3-A5 give true standard errors and 95% confidence intervals, taking account of the complex sample design, for some key variables. Since the survey used a multi-stage sample design which involved both clustering and stratification it is not appropriate to calculate standard errors using the formulae which assumes a simple random sample design.[2] Only a few of the key estimates are presented because of the large number of possible estimates which could be covered. The standard errors of other survey variables can be estimated by using the formula which assumes a simple random sample and applying a design factor of 1.1 in England.

Tables A3-A5

References

1. Barton J and Jarvis L. S*moking among secondary school children in 1996: Scotland* , 1997 (London: The Stationery Office)

2. The calculation of the standard errors and design factors presented uses the package EPSILON which was developed by Social Survey Division for samples drawn using multi-stage sample designs. For further details of the method of calculation see Butcher B and Elliot D. *A sampling errors manual*, 1987 (London: OPCS)

Table A1 Allocation of primary sampling units to strata

England 1996

Type of school		Population	Estimated PSUs	Actual PSUs
LEA comprehensive	Boys	54.258	2.41	2
	Girls	88,325	3.93	4
	Mixed	1,905,980	84.72	85
LEA selective	All	41,137	1.83	2
LEA modern	All	70,697	3.14	3
Grant maintained comprehensive	Boys	31,180	1.39	1
	Girls	24,726	1.10	1
	Mixed	358,502	15.93	16
Grant maintained selective	Boys	23,143	1.03	1
	Girls	15,832	0.70	1
	Mixed	14,120	0.63	1
Grant maintained modern	All	31,797	1.41	1
Independent selective	Boys	47,940	2.13	2
	Girls	59,331	2.64	3
	Mixed	76,962	3.42	3
Independent non-selective	All	35,825	1.59	2
Total		**2,879,755**		**128**

Table A2 Quota sizes and maximum sample sizes expected in selected schools in each stratum

England 1996

Type of school		Schools	Quota size	Maximum sample
LEA comprehensive	Boys	2	27	54
	Girls	4	29	116
	Mixed	85	29	2465
LEA selective	All	2	31	62
LEA modern	All	3	27	81
Grant maintained comprehensive	Boys	1	31	31
	Girls	1	25	25
	Mixed	16	29	464
Grant maintained selective	Boys	1	35	35
	Girls	1	24	24
	Mixed	1	42	42
Grant maintained modern	All	1	32	32
Independent selective	Boys	2	29	58
	Girls	3	30	90
	Mixed	3	29	87
Independent non-selective	All	2	27	54
Total		**128**		**3720**

Table A3 True standard errors and 95% confidence intervals for smoking behaviour

England 1996

Base	Characteristic	%(p)	Sample size	True standard error of p	95% confidence interval	Deft
	Smoking behaviour					
Boys	Regular smoker	10.7	1445	0.92	8.9 - 12.5	1.14
	Occasional smoker	7.6	1445	0.76	6.1 - 9.1	1.09
	Used to smoke	7.4	1445	0.82	5.8 - 9.0	1.20
	Tried smoking once	21.6	1445	1.28	19.1 - 24.1	1.18
	Has never smoked	52.7	1445	1.47	49.8 - 55.6	1.12
Girls	Regular smoker	14.8	1409	0.97	12.9 - 16.7	1.02
	Occasional smoker	10.0	1409	0.84	8.4 - 11.6	1.05
	Used to smoke	9.1	1409	0.69	7.8 - 10.4	0.89
	Tried smoking once	17.7	1409	1.00	15.7 - 19.7	0.99
	Has never smoked	48.4	1409	1.46	45.5 - 51.3	1.10
Total	Regular smoker	12.7	2854	0.70	11.3 - 14.1	1.13
	Occasional smoker	8.8	2854	0.59	7.6 - 10.0	1.11
	Used to smoke	8.2	2854	0.58	7.1 - 9.3	1.13
	Tried smoking once	19.7	2854	0.91	17.9 - 21.5	1.23
	Has never smoked	50.6	2854	1.11	48.4 - 52.8	1.19

Table A4   True standard errors and 95% confidence intervals for current smokers by age

England 1996

Base	Characteristic	%(p)	Sample size	True standard error of p	95% confidence interval	Deft
	Smoking behaviour					
Age 11	Regular smoker	0.9	546	0.41	0.1 - 1.7	1.00
	Occasional smoker	3.8	546	0.99	1.9 - 5.7	1.20
Age 12	Regular smoker	3.0	575	0.62	1.8 - 4.2	0.88
	Occasional smoker	5.4	575	0.96	3.5 - 7.3	1.01
Age 13	Regular smoker	9.6	560	1.17	7.3 - 11.9	0.94
	Occasional smoker	10.4	560	1.55	7.4 - 13.4	1.20
Age 14	Regular smoker	18.4	586	1.91	14.7 - 22.1	1.19
	Occasional smoker	11.4	586	1.15	9.2 - 13.6	0.88
Age 15	Regular smoker	30.5	587	1.73	27.1 - 33.9	0.91
	Occasional smoker	12.6	587	1.20	10.2 - 15.0	0.88

Table A5   True standard errors and 95% confidence intervals for consumption

England 1996

Base	Characteristic	Mean	Sample size	True standard error of mean	95% confidence interval	Deft
	Smoking behaviour					
Boys	Regular smoker	55.8	154	3.80	48.3 - 63.4	0.76
	Occasional smoker	8.2	107	1.61	4.9 - 11.4	1.07
	All smokers	36.3	261	2.62	31.1 - 41.5	0.79
	All boys	6.6	1442	0.66	5.3 - 7.9	0.93
Girls	Regular smoker	47.3	208	2.53	42.4 - 52.4	0.95
	Occasional smoker	5.4	141	0.85	3.7 - 7.1	0.81
	All smokers	30.4	349	1.83	26.8 - 34.0	0.92
	All girls	7.5	1408	0.57	6.4 - 8.6	0.94
Total	Regular smoker	50.9	362	2.26	46.5 - 55.4	0.86
	Occasional smoker	6.6	248	0.87	4.9 - 8.3	0.99
	All smokers	32.9	610	1.55	29.9 - 35.0	0.85
	All pupils	7.0	2850	0.45	6.2 - 7.9	0.98

Appendix B **Classification of smoking behaviour**

The fivefold classification used in this series of surveys is based on a combination of information from the self-completion questionnaire and the smoking diary. It was developed by ONS in consultation with various experts in the field of children's smoking, and was discussed in some detail in the report on the 1982 survey. In this appendix smoking behaviour according to the questionnaire and the diary is looked at in the light of the additional information from the saliva test (first introduced on the 1988 survey and then repeated in the rest of the series).

Smoking behaviour according to the questionnaire

The prevalence question is in two parts, a main question followed by a check question for those who said at the main question that they had never smoked, as shown in Figure B1.

In 1996, in answer to the main question, 55% of pupils said that they had never smoked, but at the check question, 7% of this group admitted that they had actually tried smoking.

The replies to the main question and the check question have been combined to provide a classification of pupils' smoking behaviour according to their answers on the questionnaire. Those who at the check question admitted to having had a puff or two of a cigarette have been classified as having tried smoking once. Three pupils who at the main question said they had never smoked said at the check question that they did sometimes smoke cigarettes. Table B1 shows that using the combined measure, the proportion of pupils saying they had never smoked falls to 51%. The proportion who, at the date of the survey, had apparently experimented only briefly with cigarettes rises to 21%.

Table B1, Figure B1

Figure B1

6. Now read all the following statements carefully and tick the box next to the one which best describes you.

    I have never smoked ☐ 1 — **Go to Question 7**

    I have only ever tried smoking once ☐ 2

    I used to smoke sometimes but I never smoke a cigarette now ☐ 3 — **Go to Question 8**

    I sometimes smoke cigarettes now but I don't smoke as many as one a week ☐ 4 — **Go to Question 14**

    I usually smoke between one and six cigarettes a week ☐ 5

    I usually smoke more than six cigarettes a week ☐ 6 — **Go to Question 9**

---

7. Just to check, read the statements below carefully and tick the box next to the one which best describes you.

    I have never tried smoking a cigarette, not even a puff or two ☐ 1

    I did once have a puff or two of a cigarette, but I never smoke now ☐ 2 — **Go to Question 8**

    I do sometimes smoke cigarettes ☐ 3 — **Go to Question 14**

Smoking behaviour according to the diary

In addition to the questionnaire, pupils also completed a diary covering the previous seven days. Each day was divided into six broad periods: early morning, morning, dinner time, afternoon, teatime and evening. For each period, for each of the previous seven days, pupils were asked a question about what they had been doing at that time, and were asked to record how many cigarettes, if any, they had smoked. All pupils were asked to complete the diary, whatever they had said about their smoking in answer to the prevalence question.

A combined classification of smoking behaviour, based on information from both the prevalence question and the diary, has been used throughout the series of surveys. The intention of this classification is to distinguish between children who are regular smokers, even if infrequent ones, and those who are not. It is based on answers to the prevalence question, except that those who say at the prevalence question that they are not smokers but record cigarettes on the diary are classified as occasional smokers (irrespective of the number of cigarettes recorded). The full classification of smoking behaviour is shown in Figure B2.

Figure B2

Table B2 shows the number of cigarettes recorded on the diary for pupils classified by their responses at the prevalence question. Complete consistency between the two sets of answers would not be expected, because the prevalence questions asked about usual behaviour for current smokers, whereas the diary related to what was smoked in the previous week. However, as in previous surveys, regular smokers seem to have underestimated how much they smoked at the prevalence question. For example, 72% of those who said that they usually smoked between one and six cigarettes a week had recorded seven or more cigarettes on the diary as being smoked last week. This is not of major importance to the survey finding, because it did not affect their classification as regular smokers, which depended only on their saying that they smoke at least one cigarette a week at the prevalence question.

However similar under-reporting seems to have occurred among the group of children who said that they did smoke, but not as many as one a week. One in five children (20%) had apparently smoked on average one or more cigarettes a day in the previous week. This suggests that some children who are probably regular smokers (according to the definition we are using) have been classified as occasional smokers. It is possible that this included pupils who had a smoking 'session' during the diary week, but because they had not smoked for several weeks previous to this, described themselves on the questionnaire as smoking less than one cigarette a week.

Table B2

The inconsistencies noted between answers at the prevalence question and cigarettes recorded on the diary are in most cases unlikely to result from children deliberately giving inconsistent answers. Surveys of smoking among adults have found that they, too, underestimate cigarette consumption - there may be a natural tendency to do so, particularly when asked to estimate the number of cigarettes smoked over a period. In addition, some children may have had difficulty with the concepts of present and past behaviour

Figure B2   Fivefold classification of smoking behaviour: England, 1996

Fivefold classification	Smoking prevalence question	Diary	Number of pupils
Regular smoker	usually smokes more than 6 cigs	cigs	260
	usually smokes more than 6 cigs	no cigs	4
	usually smokes 1-6 cigs a week	cigs	93
	usually smokes 1-6 cigs a week	no cigs	6
Occasional smoker	smoked sometimes	cigs	112
	smoked sometimes	no cigs	50
	used to smoke	cigs	45
	tried smoking once	cigs	38
	never smoked	cigs	6
Used to smoke	used to smoke	no cigs	235
Tried smoking once	tried smoking once	no cigs	561
Has never smoked	never smoked	no cigs	1444

underlying the prevalence question; these may tend to imply the more stable, settled pattern of adult life rather than the more erratic, experimental behaviour of some children.

The lack of correspondence between self-reported smoking on the questionnaire and the diary suggests that the 'occasional smoker' category is not a distinct one. At a period in children's lives when smoking behaviour is constantly changing the composition of this group is also very unstable. The number of cigarettes recorded on the diary for children in each category of the full prevalence classification is shown in Table B3.

Table B3

The saliva test

Saliva testing was first introduced in the 1988 survey. The main purpose of including this procedure was to try to validate the estimates of prevalence obtained from the questionnaire and the diary. A separate hypothesis was that saliva testing would affect reporting behaviour - that is, that children tend to under-report their smoking, so the addition of saliva testing might be expected to increase reported prevalence rates by encouraging children to be more honest.

The procedure used for obtaining saliva specimens

The saliva specimens were obtained while pupils were filling in the questionnaires and diaries. The pupils were fully aware of the purpose of the procedure; the interviewer told them that it was to measure the amount of nicotine in their bodies. He or she also explained that it was not only smokers who would have nicotine in their saliva, but that being in a smoky room or even just sitting next to a smoker on the bus could affect the level of nicotine in the body.

Pupils were given a small tube containing a dental roll, and asked to put the latter in the mouth between the cheek and the gum, and to leave it there without chewing it (which reduces the amount of saliva retained) while they filled in the questionnaire and the diary. After twenty minutes, they were told to take out the dental roll and put it back in the labelled tube. The specimens were subsequently sent to the Health Behaviour Unit at the University College London Medical School for analysis by gas chromatography.

Cotinine is a major metabolite of nicotine. It has a half-life in saliva of 16-20 hours, and so reflects exposure to tobacco smoke over the past few days. Its sensitivity is such that very low levels of exposure, such as might result from passive smoking (inhaling smoke from tobacco smoked by someone else) can be detected. In the remainder of this chapter, cotinine levels are compared with self-reported smoking behaviour, in order to assess the accuracy of the estimates of prevalence.

The effects of the saliva test on estimates of the prevalence of smoking

It might be expected that saliva testing would affect the reporting of current smoking behaviour, in that it might increase self-reported smoking, but would be less likely to affect the proportion saying that they had never smoked at all. In the 1988 survey, the saliva test did seem to have an effect, but in the subsequent surveys between 1990 and 1994 there was no difference between the test and control samples in the reported prevalence of smoking.

However, in 1996, the reported prevalence of cigarette smoking was higher in the test sample than in the control sample. Fourteen per cent of the test group reported that they were regular smokers compared with 11% in the control group. There was also a difference in the proportion reporting that they had never smoked - 46% of the test group and 55% of the control group said they had never smoked.

When boys and girls are considered separately, the saliva test appears to have a greater effect on reported prevalence among boys, increasing the estimate from nine per cent to thirteen per cent, whilst among girls the increase from 14% to 16% was not statistically significant. Conversely, the effect of the saliva test on whether the pupils said they had never smoked was greater among girls than among boys (42% of girls in the test group said they had never smoked compared with 55% of the control group).

Table B4

As this is the first time that there has been a difference in prevalence between the saliva test and control groups since 1988, it was thought unlikely that the test had affected the reporting of cigarette smoking and that instead there may have been slight differences in the characteristics of the two samples. Although the splitting of the sample of schools was controlled, so that the subsamples were well matched, it was not possible to control the number of boys and girls selected in each school. Thus some differences between the test and control samples would be expected, simply from random sampling variation.

Those in the test sample were slightly older on average than those in the control sample, which would tend to increase overall prevalence among those tested relative to those not tested. Table B6 shows that among boys a higher prevalence in the test sample was evident in the older age groups, which would suggest that there is an effect of the saliva sample independent of the age of the two groups. To control for this effect of age, age-standardised data was produced: an expected prevalence was calculated for saliva and non-saliva schools which was what would have been obtained if the prevalence rates in each age group were the same for that type of school as in the whole sample.

Tables B5-B6

When age is controlled for, there is no statistically significant difference between the test or control group in the proportion of regular smokers. This would suggest that the saliva test does not have an effect on reported smoking independent of age. However, there is still a lower proportion of pupils in the test group compared with the control group reporting that they had never smoked.

Table B7

Cotinine levels and self-reported smoking behaviour

When saliva is analysed for the presence of cotinine, the amounts found range from undetectable - less than 0.1 nanogram per millilitre (ng/ml) - to over 400 ng/ml. Clearly, at the extremes of this range, pupils were definitely non-smokers or definitely smokers. However, there is a range of cotinine values which could be due to either passive or active smoking. On the one hand, non-smoking children may have cotinine concentrations raised through exposure to other people's smoke, and on the other, some self-reported smokers may not have smoked in the last few days, or may not inhale. This means that cotinine concentrations cannot distinguish between smokers and non-smokers with complete accuracy, particularly when, as with the present survey, some of the children are in the early phases of experimentation with cigarettes.

Table B8 gives summary information on cotinine levels for pupils in each category of the combined smoking classification based on both the questionnaire and the diary - i.e. the classification which is used throughout this report to provide estimates of prevalence. The average, or mean, cotinine level on its own is not always very helpful; a few pupils with particularly high levels can have a disproportionate effect on its value. Thus the table also shows the median value and the lower and upper quartiles, as these are often better indicators of central tendency where the data are highly skewed. The medians and interquartile ranges, together with outlying values, are plotted in Figure B3.

As in previous surveys, the table and figure show that the level of correspondence between the saliva cotinine value and the pupils' self-reported smoking behaviour was good. As would be expected there is a very large difference between the mean for regular smokers and all the other four groups of pupils.

Figure B3 shows no outlying values for regular smokers - they are inappropriate for this group, because all values, no matter how high or low, are consistent with being a regular smoker. This is obviously the case for high values, but some very low cotinine levels are also to be expected, because of the low threshold for being defined as a regular smoker (usually smoking one cigarette a week), which means that some pupils classified as regular smokers will not have smoked at all in the last few days.

Pharmacokinetic considerations and empirical work on other studies where cotinine has been used as a marker for cigarette smoking[1] suggest that it is virtually impossible for a saliva cotinine level greater than 20 ng/ml to be due solely to passive smoking. Therefore all pupils who say they are non-smokers whose saliva cotinine is above this level can be assumed to be lying and are shown as outliers on the chart. Of those who said that they were not smokers, a maximum of three out of about 600 pupils in these three groups were untruthful. Two of them were regular smokers with cotinine levels of over 70 ng/ml and one was probably an occasional smoker.

It is also unlikely that saliva cotinine levels over about 40 ng/ml would be found in someone who only smoked occasionally, so self-reported occasional smokers with levels higher than this could be

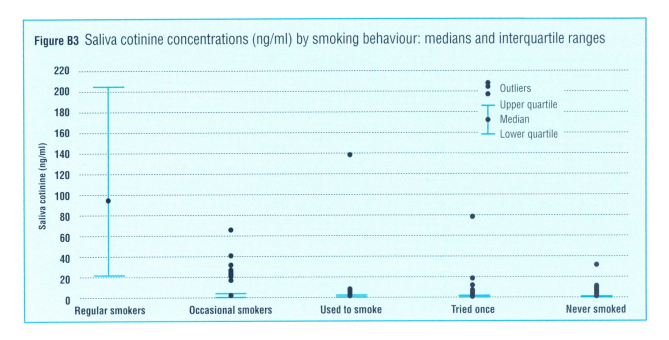

Figure B3 Saliva cotinine concentrations (ng/ml) by smoking behaviour: medians and interquartile ranges

assumed to be understating their consumption. Pupils with saliva cotinine concentrations less than 20 ng/ml may also be lying about their smoking, but this is impossible to determine, because low cotinine levels can be found both in passive smokers and in occasional smokers. Figure B3 shows that only one pupil classified as an occasional smoker has a cotinine level (65 ng/ml) which would suggest that she is a regular smoker.

If these pupils were reclassified on the basis of their saliva tests, the prevalence rates would remain unchanged.

Table B8 Figure B3

Cotinine levels and exposure to tobacco smoke last week

Although a detailed analysis of the relationship between cigarette consumption and saliva cotinine concentration is beyond the scope of this report, Table B9 presents summary data for pupils classified according to their probable exposure to cigarette smoke in the previous week. Those who had smoked during the previous week (i.e. those who had recorded cigarettes on the diary) were categorised according to how many cigarettes they said they had smoked, and those who had not smoked were classified according to the smoking behaviour of their parent(s). Pupils who lived with only one parent were classified according to the smoking behaviour of that parent. Self-reported non-smokers with saliva cotinine levels greater than 20 ng/ml were excluded from the analysis as it seemed likely that they had smoked in the last week.

Table B9 shows a striking variation in saliva cotinine concentration, and hence, nicotine intake, according to the number of cigarettes smoked in the previous week. The mean concentration of saliva cotinine for those who smoked on average more than 10 cigarettes a day last week was 196 ng/ml compared with only 8 ng/ml for those who had smoked less than one cigarette a day. The cotinine values of those who had smoked more than 10 cigarettes a day, on average, were very similar to those found in adult smokers (very few of whom smoke less than this). This adds weight to the suggestion that children who smoke are just as likely to inhale when they smoke as are adults.[2]

Parental smoking is, of course, only a very rough guide to exposure to passive smoking, which may also arise from a variety of other sources. Nonetheless, the concentration of cotinine in the saliva of non-smoking children is clearly related to whether one or both of their parents smoke. The strength of the association is particularly striking in view of the limited time each week that most schoolchildren spend with their parents. Those children in families where no parent smoked had very low concentrations of saliva cotinine. If one parent was a smoker, the cotinine levels were significantly higher, particularly if it was the pupil's mother who smoked. If both parents were smokers, cotinine levels were more than five times greater than if neither parent smoked.

Table B9

When the smoking behaviour of pupils' siblings was considered, the mean cotinine level of non-smoking children who had siblings who smoked was higher than that of those whose siblings did not smoke.

Table B10

References

1. Jarvis MJ. Uptake of environmental tobacco smoke. In: O'Neill I K et al (eds).*Environmental carcinogens: methods of analysis and exposure measurement, Vol 9 Passive smoking.* International Agency for Research on Cancer - Scientific Publication No. 1 (Lyon, 1987)

2. McNeill AD, Jarvis MJ, West R, Russell MAH, and Bryant A. Saliva cotinine as an indication of cigarette smoking in adolescence, *British Journal of Addiction,* 1987; 82, pp 1355-60

Table B1   Replies to prevalence and check question
All pupils   *England 1996*

	Prevalence question	Check question	Both combined
	%	%	%
I have never smoked	55	93	51
I have only smoked once	17	7	21
I used to smoke sometimes, but I never smoke now	10		10
I sometimes smoked cigarettes now, but I don't smoke as many as one a week	6	0	6
I usually smoke between one and six cigarettes a week	3		3
I usually smoke more than six cigarettes a week	9		9
Base (=100%)	*2854*	*1548*	*2854*

Table B2   Cigarettes recorded on the diary, by smoking behaviour according to the questionnaire
All pupils   *England 1996*

Cigarettes on diary	Usually smokes			Used to smoke	Tried smoking	Never smoked	Total
	More than 6 a week	1-6 a week	Less than 1 a week				
	%	%	%	%	%	%	%
None	2	6	31	85	94	100	81
1-6	2	21	49	11	5	-	6
7-70	62	71	19	4	2	-	10
71 or more	34	1	1	-	-	-	3
Base (=100%)	*264*	*98*	*161*	*278*	*599*	*1450*	*2850*

Table B3   Cigarettes recorded on the diary, by smoking behaviour according to the fivefold classification
All pupils   *England 1996*

Cigarettes on diary	Regular smoker	Occasional smoker	Used to smoke	Tried smoking	Never smoked	Total
	%	%	%	%	%	%
None	3	20	100	100	100	81
1-6	7	56	-	-	-	6
7-70	65	22	-	-	-	10
71 or more	25	2	-	-	-	3
Base (=100%)	*362*	*248*	*235*	*561*	*1444*	*2850*

Table B4   Smoking behaviour by sex and whether in test or control group sample
All pupils   *England 1996*

Smoking behaviour	Boys		Girls		Total	
	Test	Control	Test	Control	Test	Control
	%	%	%	%	%	%
Regular smoker	13	9	16	14	14	11
Occasional smoker	8	7	12	8	10	8
Used to smoke	8	7	11	8	9	7
Tried smoking	22	21	20	16	21	19
Never smoked	50	56	42	55	46	55
Base (=100%)	*754*	*691*	*680*	*729*	*1434*	*1420*

Table B5 Age by sex and whether in test or control sample

All pupils   *England 1996*

Age	Boys Test	Control	Girls Test	Control	Total Test	Control
	%	%	%	%	%	%
11 years	18	19	17	22	18	21
12 years	18	23	17	22	18	23
13 years	19	20	21	19	20	19
14 years	22	20	24	17	23	18
15 years	23	18	21	20	22	19
Base (=100%)	*754*	*691*	*680*	*729*	*1434*	*1420*

Table B6 Prevalence of regular cigarette smoking, by sex, age and whether in test or control sample

All pupils   *England 1996*

Age	Boys Test	Control	Girls Test	Control	Total Test	Control
	% of regular smokers					
11 years	2	1	1	0	2	0
12 years	1	3	3	4	2	4
13 years	8	9	11	12	9	10
14 years	16	9	25	23	21	16
15 years	31	23	34	33	32	29
Total	13	9	16	14	14	11
Bases (=100%)						
11 years	*138*	*134*	*116*	*158*	*254*	*292*
12 years	*138*	*159*	*114*	*164*	*252*	*323*
13 years	*143*	*139*	*142*	*136*	*285*	*275*
14 years	*163*	*135*	*163*	*125*	*326*	*260*
15 years	*172*	*124*	*145*	*146*	*317*	*270*
Total	*754*	*691*	*680*	*729*	*1434*	*1420*

Table B7 Age-standardised prevalence of regular cigarette smoking and those who have never smoked, by sex and whether in test or control sample

All pupils   *England 1996*

	Boys Test	Control	Girls Test	Control	Total Test	Control
Regular smokers	11.8	9.1	14.9	14.7	13.3	11.9
Never smoked	50.7	55.6	43.7	53.0	47.3	54.2
Base (=100%)	*754*	*691*	*680*	*729*	*1434*	*1420*

Table B8 Summary indicators of saliva cotinine levels, by self-reported smoking behaviour

Pupils in the saliva test sample   *England 1996*

Saliva cotinine	Regular smoker	Occasional smoker	Used to smoke	Tried smoking	Never smoked	Total
Mean	121.8	5.6	3.3	1.9	1.2	19.9
(st dev)	(112.1)	(11.2)	(15.4)	(6.5)	(2.3)	(61.0)
Minimum	0.1	0.1	0.0	0.0	0.0	0.0
Lower quartile	22.4	0.5	0.5	0.3	0.2	0.3
Median	93.8	1.2	1.0	0.7	0.4	0.8
Upper quartile	205.4	4.2	2.4	1.7	1.4	3.2
Maximum	446.9	65.1	139.1	79.2	30.8	446.9
Base(=100%)	*116*	*68*	*80*	*160*	*356*	*780*

Table B9   Saliva cotinine levels, by whether active or passive smoker

Pupils in the saliva test sample   *England 1996*

Saliva cotinine (ng/ml)	Smoked last week			Did not smoke last week*			
	More than 70 cigarettes	7-70 cigarettes	1-6 cigarettes	Two parents smoke	Mother only smokes	Father only smokes	No parent smokes
Mean	[196.5]	88.8	[7.9]	3.3	2.5	1.1	0.6
(st dev)	[(105.5)]	(96.6)	[(22.3)]	(2.4)	(2.5)	(0.9)	(1.2)
Minimum	[25.0]	0.1	[0.1]	0.0	0.0	0.0	0.0
Lower quartile	[105.6]	6.8	[0.4]	1.4	0.8	0.4	0.1
Median	[185.1]	48.7	[1.0]	2.7	2.0	0.9	0.3
Upper quartile	[268.5]	151.9	[4.1]	4.8	3.3	1.4	0.6
Maximum	[446.9]	335.1	[133.6]	10.0	18.4	4.2	17.9
Base	*31*	*85*	*48*	*69*	*100*	*97*	*321*

* Pupils who live with only one parent have been categorised according to the smoking behaviour of that parent; pupils who said they did not smoke in the last week with cotinine levels of more than 20 ng/ml have been excluded

Table B10   Saliva cotinine levels for passive smokers by siblings smoking

Non-smoking pupils in the saliva test sample   *England 1996*

Saliva cotinine	Did not smoke last week*			
	Has at least one sibling who smokes	Has no siblings who smoke	Has no siblings living at home	Can't be sure of siblings' smoking behaviour
Mean	1.9	1.2	1.7	1.1
(st dev)	(2.0)	(1.8)	(2.7)	(1.5)
Minimum	0.0	0.0	0.0	0.0
Lower quartile	0.5	0.2	0.3	0.2
Median	1.3	0.5	0.6	0.6
Upper quartile	2.9	1.4	2.2	1.5
Maximum	10.2	18.4	17.9	9.0
Base	*93*	*314*	*65*	*136*

* Excludes pupils with cotinine levels of more than 20 ng/ml

Appendix C **The self-completion documents**

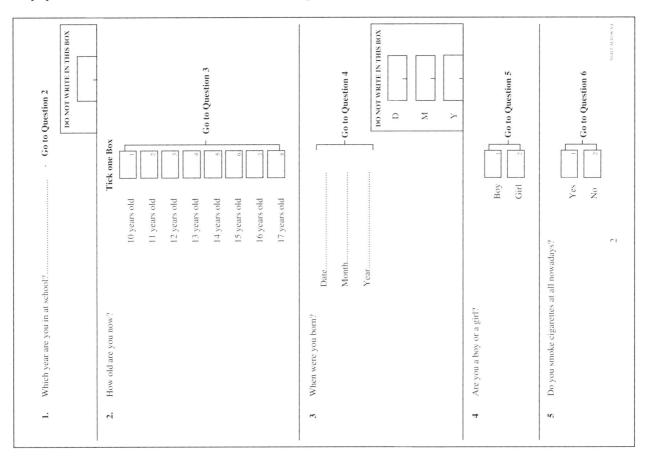

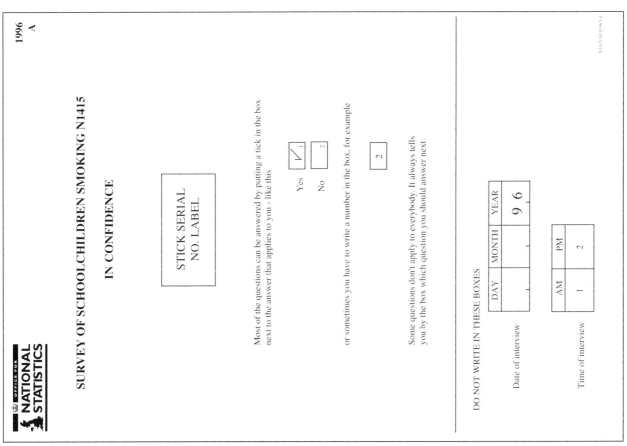

6. Now read all the following statements carefully and tick the box next to the one which best describes you.

I have never smoked □1 → **Go to Question 7**

I have only ever tried smoking once □2
I used to smoke sometimes but I never smoke a cigarette now □3 → **Go to Question 8**

I sometimes smoke cigarettes now but I don't smoke as many as one a week □4 → **Go to Question 14**

I usually smoke between one and six cigarettes a week □5 → **Go to Question 9**
I usually smoke more than six cigarettes a week □6

7. Just to check, read the statements below carefully and tick the box next to the one which best describes you.

I have never tried smoking a cigarette, not even a puff or two □1 → **Go to Question 8**
I did once have a puff or two of a cigarette, but I never smoke now □2

I do sometimes smoke cigarettes □3 → **Go to Question 14**

8. How do you think your family would feel if you started smoking?

They would stop me □1
They would try to persuade me not to smoke □2
They would do nothing □3 → **Go to Question 19**
They would encourage me to smoke □4
I don't know □5

3

9. How long is it since you started smoking at least one cigarette a week?

Less than 3 months □1
3 - 6 months □2
6 months to 1 year □3
more than one year □4 → **Go to Question 10**

10. How easy or difficult would you find it to go without smoking for as long as a week?

Very difficult □1
Fairly difficult □2
Fairly easy □3
Very easy □4 → **Go to Question 11**

11. How easy or difficult would you find it to give up smoking altogether if you wanted to?

Very difficult □1
Fairly difficult □2
Fairly easy □3
Very easy □4 → **Go to Question 12**

12. Would you like to give up smoking altogether?

Yes □1
No □2 → **Go to Question 13**
I don't know □3

13. Have you ever tried to give up smoking?

Yes □1
No □2 → **Go to Question 14**

4

14. How does your family feel about you smoking?

They stop me ☐ 1

They try to persuade me not to smoke ☐ 2

They do nothing ☐ 3

They encourage me to smoke ☐ 4

They don't know I smoke ☐ 5

I don't know ☐ 6

Go to Question 15

15. Are you allowed to smoke at home if you want to?

Yes ☐ 1

No ☐ 2

I don't know ☐ 3

Go to Question 16

16. Where do you **usually** get your cigarettes from? (Please tick more than one box if you **often** get cigarettes from different people or places.)

I buy them from a supermarket ☐ 1

I buy them from a newsagent, tobacconist or sweet shop ☐ 2

I buy them from a garage shop ☐ 3

I buy them from some other type of shop ☐ 4

I buy them from a machine ☐ 5

I buy them from other people ☐ 6

Friends give them to me ☐ 7

My brother or sister gives them to me ☐ 8

My mother or father gives them to me ☐ 9

I take them ☐ 10

I get them in some other way ☐ 11

Go to Question 17

17. On the whole, do you find it easy or difficult to buy cigarettes from a shop?

Very difficult ☐ 1

Fairly difficult ☐ 2

Fairly easy ☐ 3

Very easy ☐ 4

I don't usually buy cigarettes from a shop ☐ 5

Go to Question 18

18. How old were you when you first tried smoking a cigarette, even if it was only a puff or two? Write in the box your **age then**, in numbers, not words.

I was [ ] years old - **Go to Question 19**

Now, thinking about your family, that is the people you live with at home:

19. Do you live with your mother?
(You should also answer "Yes" if you live with your stepmother or adopted mother.)

Yes ☐ 1   **Go to Question 19a**

No ☐ 2   **Go to Question 20**

19a. Does she smoke?

Yes ☐ 1

No ☐ 2

Go to Question 20

20. Do you live with your father?
(You should also answer "Yes" if you live with your stepfather or adopted father.)

Yes ☐ 1   **Go to Question 20a**

No ☐ 2   **Go to Question 21**

20a. Does he smoke?

Yes ☐ 1

No ☐ 2

Go to Question 21

21. How many brothers or sisters do you have **living at home** with you?
(If you haven't any brothers or sisters, write in '0' in each box and miss out Question 22)

Write a number (0,1,2...) in each box

Number of older brothers ☐ 1
Number of older sisters ☐ 2
Number of younger brothers ☐ 3
Number of younger sisters ☐ 4

→ Go to Question 22

22. How many of them are smokers?

Write a number (0,1,2...) in each box

	Number who smoke	Number who don't smoke	Number I'm not sure about
Older brothers	☐ 1	☐ 2	☐ 3
Older sisters	☐ 1	☐ 2	☐ 3
Younger brothers	☐ 1	☐ 2	☐ 3
Younger sisters	☐ 1	☐ 2	☐ 3

→ Go to Question 23

23. Is there anyone else living at home with you who smokes?

Yes ☐ 1
No ☐ 2

→ Go to Question 24

24. What about your friends - how many of them smoke?

All of them ☐ 1
Most but not all ☐ 2
Half and half ☐ 3
Only a few ☐ 4
None of them smoke ☐ 5

→ Go to Question 25

7

25. In the last year, has anyone in your family talked to you about the effects of smoking on your health?

Yes ☐ 1
No ☐ 2

→ Go to Question 26

26. In the last year, has anyone in your family talked to you about the effects of breathing in other people's smoke (called passive smoking) on your health?

Yes ☐ 1
No ☐ 2

→ Go to Question 27

27. Below are a few things people say about smoking. Some people think they are true and some people think they are not true. What do you think?

Against each sentence tick one box to show if you think it is true or false

TICK ONE BOX

	TRUE	NOT TRUE
a. Smoking gives people confidence	☐ 1	☐ 2
b. Smoking makes people worse at sports	☐ 1	☐ 2
c. Smokers stay slimmer than non-smokers	☐ 1	☐ 2
d. If a woman smokes when she is pregnant it can harm her unborn baby	☐ 1	☐ 2
e. Smoking helps people relax if they feel nervous	☐ 1	☐ 2
f. Smoking can cause heart disease	☐ 1	☐ 2
g. Smoking is not really dangerous, it only harms people who smoke a lot	☐ 1	☐ 2
h. Smokers get more coughs and colds than non-smokers	☐ 1	☐ 2
i. Other people's smoking can harm the health of non-smokers	☐ 1	☐ 2
j. Smoking helps people cope better with life	☐ 1	☐ 2
k. Smoking makes your clothes smell	☐ 1	☐ 2
l. Smokers are more fun than non-smokers	☐ 1	☐ 2
m. Smoking can cause lung cancer	☐ 1	☐ 2

→ Go to Question 28

8

28. In the past year, have you ever gone **into a shop** to buy cigarettes? This includes buying cigarettes for somebody else.

Yes ☐1 — **Go to Question 29**

No ☐2 — **Go to Question 34**

29. At **any** of these times when you went into a shop to buy cigarettes, did the shopkeeper refuse to sell them to you?

Yes ☐1

No ☐2 — **Go to Question 30**

30. The **last** time you went into a shop to buy cigarettes, what happened?

I bought some cigarettes ☐1 — **Go to Question 31**

They refused to sell me any cigarettes ☐2 — **Go to Question 33**

31. How many cigarettes did you buy last time? Write the **number** in the box.

I bought ☐ cigarettes - **Go to Question 32**

32. Did you buy them for yourself or for someone else?

For myself ☐1

For my mother ☐2

For my father ☐3

For my brother or sister ☐4 — **Go to Question 33**

For a friend ☐5

For someone else ☐6

33. How often do you buy cigarettes **from a shop**?

Almost every day ☐1

Once or twice a week ☐2

Two or three times a month ☐3

About once a month ☐4

Only a few times a year ☐5 — **Go to Question 34**

34. How often do you buy cigarettes **from a machine**?

Almost every day ☐1

Once or twice a week ☐2

Two or three times a month ☐3

About once a month ☐4

Only a few times a year ☐5

Never buy from machine ☐6 — **Go to Question 35**

35. How much money of your own do you have most weeks to spend as you like?

- Nothing □1 — **Go to Question 37**
- Less than £1 a week □2
- £1 or more but less than £5 □3
- £5 or more but less than £10 □4 — **Go to Question 36**
- £10 or more but less than £20 □5
- £20 or more a week □6

36. Does this money come from —

You may tick more than one box

- pocket money □1 — **Go to Question 37**
- paid work outside school hours □2
- or somewhere else? □3

37. Have you ever had a proper alcoholic drink - a whole drink, not just a sip? **Please don't count drinks labelled low alcohol.**

- Yes □1 — **Go to Question 38**
- No □2 — **Go to Question 50**

38. How old were you when you had your first proper alcoholic drink? Write in the box your **age then** in numbers, not words.

I was [ ] years old - **Go to Question 39**

11

39. How often do you **usually** have an alcoholic drink?

- Almost every day □1
- About twice a week □2
- About once a week □3
- About once a fortnight □4 — **Go to Question 40**
- About once a month □5
- Only a few times a year □6
- I never drink alcohol now □7

40. When you drink alcohol, who are you **usually** with?

- My girlfriend or boyfriend □1
- Friends of the same sex as me □2
- Friends of the opposite sex □3
- A group of friends of both sexes □4 — **Go to Question 41**
- My parents (or step-parents) □5
- My brother, sister, or other relatives □6
- On my own □7

41. And when you drink alcohol, where are you **usually**?

- In a pub or bar □1
- In a club or disco □2
- At a party with friends □3 — **Go to Question 42**
- At my home or someone else's home □4
- Somewhere else □5

12

42. If you buy alcohol, where do you **usually** buy it?

In a pub or bar ⬚ 1

In a club or disco ⬚ 2

From an off-licence ⬚ 3

From a shop or supermarket ⬚ 4

Somewhere else ⬚ 5

I never buy alcohol ⬚ 6

Go to Question 43

43. When did you **last** have an alcoholic drink?

Today ⬚ 1

Yesterday ⬚ 2

Some other time during the last week ⬚ 3

Go to Question 44

1 week, but less than 2 weeks ago ⬚ 4

2 weeks, but less than 4 weeks ago ⬚ 5

1 month, but less than 6 months ago ⬚ 6

6 months ago or more ⬚ 7

Go to Question 50

44. During the **last 7 days,** how much BEER, LAGER AND CIDER have you drunk? Please don't count drinks labelled low alcohol.

Have not drunk beer, lager or cider in the last 7 days ⬚ 1

Less than half a pint ⬚ 2

Go to Question 45

Half a pint or more ⬚ 3

Go to Question 44a

44a. Write in the boxes below the number of pints, half pints, large cans, small cans of BEER, LAGER AND CIDER drunk in the last 7 days.

Go to Question 45

pints

half pints

large cans

small cans

45. During the **last 7 days**, how much SHANDY have you drunk?

Have not drunk shandy in the last 7 days — Go to Question 46

Less than half a pint — Go to Question 46

Half a pint or more — Go to Question 45a

45a. Write in the boxes below the number of pints, half pints, large cans, small cans of SHANDY drunk in the last 7 days.

pints

half pints

large cans

small cans

Go to Question 46

46. During the **last 7 days**, how much WINE have you drunk?

Have not drunk wine in the last 7 days — Go to Question 47

Less than a glass — Go to Question 47

One glass or more — Go to Question 46a

46a. Write in the box below, the number of glasses of WINE drunk in the last 7 days.

Go to Question 47

15

47. During the **last 7 days**, how much MARTINI AND SHERRY have you drunk?

Have not drunk martini or sherry in the last 7 days — Go to Question 48

Less than a glass — Go to Question 48

One glass or more — Go to Question 47a

47a. Write in the box below, the number of glasses of MARTINI OR SHERRY drunk in the last 7 days.

Go to Question 48

48. During the **last 7 days**, how much SPIRITS (e.g. whisky, vodka, gin) AND LIQUEURS have you drunk?

By a glass we mean a single pub measure

Have not drunk spirits or liqueurs in the last 7 days — Go to Question 49

Less than a glass — Go to Question 49

One glass or more — Go to Question 48a

48a. Write in the box below, the number of glasses of SPIRITS (e.g. whisky, vodka, gin) AND LIQUEURS drunk in the last 7 days.

Go to Question 49

16

50. During the last year have you had any lessons, films or discussions in class on the following topics :

	Yes	No	Don't know
How to look after your teeth?	1	2	3
Information about exercise and sports?	1	2	3
Risks of sunbathing and sunburn?	1	2	3
Healthy eating?	1	2	3
Smoking?	1	2	3
Alcohol?	1	2	3
Sex education/safe sex?	1	2	3
AIDS?	1	2	3
Heroin?	1	2	3
Crack?	1	2	3
Solvent abuse/glue sniffing?	1	2	3
Ecstasy?	1	2	3
Drugs in general?	1	2	3

Go to Question 51

51. Do you think you will continue in full-time education after the end of year 11 (the fifth year)?

Yes ☐1
No ☐2 **Go to Question 52**
Don't know ☐3

52. Do you think you will take any GCSEs before you leave school?

Yes ☐1 **Go to Question 53**
No ☐2 **Go to Question 54**
Don't know ☐3

18

---

49. During the last 7 days, how much ALCOHOLIC LEMONADE, ALCOHOLIC COLA or OTHER ALCOHOLIC SOFT DRINKS (e.g. Hooch, Two Dogs, Lemonhead) have you drunk?

Have not drunk alcoholic lemonade, alcoholic cola or other alcoholic soft drinks in the last 7 days ☐1 **Go to Question 50**

Less than half a bottle ☐2

One bottle or more ☐3 **Go to Question 49a**

49a. Write in the boxes below the number of bottles and cans of ALCOHOLIC LEMONADE, ALCOHOLIC COLA and OTHER ALCOHOLIC SOFT DRINKS (e.g. Hooch, Two Dogs, Lemonhead) drunk in the last 7 days.

bottles ☐
cans ☐

Go to Question 50

17

58. Were there any questions you meant to go back and complete? Please check.

If you have finished, please complete the diary next, starting with yesterday and working backwards through the week.

Social Survey Division
St. Catherines House
10 Kingsway
London WC2B 6JP

20

---

53. Do you expect to get five or more passes at Grades A, B or C?

Yes [1]
No [2]
Don't know [3]
Go to Question 54

54. Does your family have a car?

Yes, two or more [1]
Yes, one [2]
No [3]
Go to Question 55

55. Does your family have a home computer? **Please don't count video games.**

Yes [1]
No [2]
Go to Question 56

56. Does your family have a dishwasher?

Yes [1]
No [2]
Go to Question 57

57. Thinking about the house or flat you live in at the moment, does your family own it or is it rented?

Own [1]
Rented [2]
Don't know [3]
Go to Question 58

19

Printed in the United Kingdom for The Stationery Office
J0025779, C8, 10/97, 5673.